LAWS AND LEGISLATION

CHILDREN'S ISSUES AND LEGISLATION

SELECT ANALYSIS AND IMPLICATIONS

LAWS AND LEGISLATION

Additional books and e-books in this series can be found on Nova's website under the Series tab.

LAWS AND LEGISLATION

CHILDREN'S ISSUES AND LEGISLATION

SELECT ANALYSIS AND IMPLICATIONS

CHRISTIE NGUYEN
EDITOR

snova
New York

Library of Congress Cataloging-in-Publication Data

ISBN: 978-1-53614-493-2

Published by Nova Science Publishers, Inc. † New York

CONTENTS

PREFACE

This book is a compilation of CRS reports on children's issues and legislation. Some topics discussed herein include runaway and homeless youth, unauthorized childhood arrivals, the Taxpayer Relief Act of 1997, the Missing Children's Assistance Act and the Deferred Action for Childhood Arrivals policy.

Chapter 1 - This report discusses runaway and homeless youth, and the federal response to support this population. There is no single definition of the terms "runaway youth" or "homeless youth." However, both groups of youth share the risk of not having adequate shelter and other provisions, and may engage in harmful behaviors while away from a permanent home. These two groups also include "thrownaway" youth who are asked to leave their homes, and may include other vulnerable youth populations, such as current and former foster youth and youth with mental health or other issues. The term "unaccompanied youth" encompasses both runaways and homeless youth, and is used in national data counts of the population.

Youth most often cite family conflict as the major reason for their homelessness or episodes of running away. A youth's sexual orientation, sexual activity, school problems, and substance abuse are associated with family discord. The precise number of homeless and runaway youth is unknown due to their residential mobility and overlap among the populations. Determining the number of these youth is further complicated by the lack of a standardized methodology for counting the population and inconsistent definitions of what it means to be homeless or a runaway. According to a federally funded study, over 4 million youth ages 13 through 25 experienced a form of homelessness over a 12-month period.

From the early 20th century through the 1960s, the needs of runaway and homeless youth were handled locally through the child welfare agency, juvenile justice courts, or both. The 1970s marked a shift toward federal oversight of programs that help youth who had run afoul of the law, including those who committed status offenses (e.g., running away). Congress and the President enacted the Runaway Youth Act of 1974 as Title III of the Juvenile Justice and Delinquency Prevention Act (P.L. 93-415) to assist runaways through services specifically for this population. These services are provided through the federal Runaway and Homeless Youth Program. The program has been updated through reauthorization laws, most recently by the Reconnecting Homeless Youth Act (P.L. 110-378) in 2008. The program is funded through the annual appropriations process. The authorization of appropriations expired in FY2013. Congress and the President have continued to provide funds for the act: $127.4 million was appropriated for FY2018.

The Runaway and Homeless Youth program is made up of three components: the Basic Center Program (BCP), Transitional Living Program (TLP), and Street Outreach Program (SOP). The Basic Center Program provides temporary shelter, counseling, and after care services to runaway and homeless youth under age 18 and their families. The BCP has served approximately 31,000 youth annually in recent years. The Transitional Living Program is targeted to older youth ages 16 through 22 (and sometimes an older age), and has served approximately 6,000 annually in recent years. Youth who use the TLP receive longer-term housing with supportive services. The SOP provides education, treatment, counseling, and referrals for runaway, homeless, and street youth who have been subjected to or are at risk of being subjected to sexual abuse, sex exploitation, and trafficking. The SOP makes contact with about 36,000 street youth annually.

Related services authorized by the Runaway and Homeless Youth Act include a national communication system to facilitate communication between service providers, runaway youth, and their families; training and technical support for grantees; and evaluations of the programs, among other activities. The 2008 reauthorization expanded the program, requiring HHS to conduct an incidence and prevalence study of runaway and homeless youth. Congress and the President provided appropriations to the U.S. Department of Housing and Urban Development (HUD) for the study, and initial findings were published in 2017. Additional efforts are underway among multiple federal agencies to collect better information on these youth as part of a larger strategy to end youth homelessness by 2020. In addition to the Runaway and Homeless Youth Program, other federal programs support runaway and homeless youth.

Chapter 2 - Legislative activity in the 115th Congress on unauthorized childhood arrivals (foreign nationals who as children were brought to live in the United States by their parents or other adults) comes in response to a decision announced by the Trump Administration on September 5, 2017, to terminate the Deferred Action for Childhood Arrivals (DACA) policy. The DACA policy was established by the Obama Administration in 2012 to provide eligible individuals with temporary protection against removal from the United States and work authorization. Initial DACA grants were for two years and could be renewed in two-year increments.

Under the Trump Administration's DACA phase-out plan announced in September 2017, a DACA beneficiary whose grant of deferred action was due to expire on or before March 5, 2018, could submit a renewal request. A beneficiary whose DACA grant was due to expire after March 5, 2018, could not request a renewal and, thus, would lose DACA protection on the grant's expiration date. As of the date of this report, however, the Department of Homeland Security (DHS) continues to process requests to renew DACA, in accordance with federal court orders. According to DHS data, as of January 31, 2018, there were approximately 682,750 active DACA recipients.

Legislative proposals on unauthorized childhood arrivals in the 115th Congress build on related legislation introduced and considered in earlier Congresses. Past measures receiving action would have established a process for eligible unauthorized childhood arrivals to become U.S. lawful permanent residents (LPRs), who can live and work permanently in the United States. None of these measures were enacted. Bills introduced in the 115th Congress include measures to provide pathways to LPR status for certain unauthorized childhood arrivals, like the bills considered in past Congresses, as well as bills to provide more-limited DACA-like temporary protection from removal and employment authorization.

In February 2018, the Senate considered three proposals on unauthorized childhood arrivals as floor amendments to an unrelated bill (H.R. 2579). Each proposal would have established a pathway to LPR status for unauthorized childhood arrivals, although there were significant differences among them with respect to the eligible population, the legalization process and timeline, and the implications for the parents of beneficiaries. The Senate rejected motions to invoke cloture on any of the amendments. The House has not considered legislation on unauthorized childhood arrivals in the 115th Congress as of the date of this report.

Chapter 3 - The child tax credit was initially structured in the Taxpayer Relief Act of 1997 (P.L. 105-34) as a $500-per-child nonrefundable credit to provide tax relief to middle- and upper-middle-income families. Since 1997, various laws have modified key parameters of the credit, expanding the availability of the benefit to more low-income families while also increasing the value of the tax credit. The first significant change to the child tax credit occurred with the enactment of the Economic Growth and Tax Relief Reconciliation Act of 2001 (EGTRRA; P.L. 107-16). EGTRRA increased the amount of the credit over time to $1,000 per child and made it partially refundable under the earned income formula. The refundable portion of the credit—the amount that exceeds income tax liability—is often referred to as the additional child tax credit or ACTC.

Subsequent legislation enacted in 2003 and 2004 accelerated the implementation of the changes made under EGTRRA. In 2008 and 2009, Congress passed legislation—the Emergency Economic Stabilization Act of 2008 (EESA; P.L. 110-343) and the American Recovery and Reinvestment Act of 2009 (ARRA; P.L. 111-5)—that further expanded the availability and amount of the credit to taxpayers whose income was too low to either qualify for the credit or be eligible for the full credit. ARRA lowered the refundability threshold to its current level of $3,000 for 2009 through 2010. The ARRA provisions were subsequently extended several times and made permanent by the Protecting Americans from Tax Hikes (PATH) Act of 2015 (Division Q of P.L. 114-113).

At the end of 2017, Congress enacted P.L. 115-97 which, in addition to making numerous changes to the tax code, temporarily changed the child tax credit. Specifically, the law increased the credit for many (though not all) taxpayers by doubling the maximum amount of the credit (and increasing the maximum amount of the ACTC to $1,400), increasing the income at which the credit begins to phase out, and reducing the refundability threshold. In addition, this law temporarily modified the identification (ID) number requirement of the credit, requiring taxpayers to provide the Social Security number (SSN) for every child for whom they claimed the credit.

P.L. 115-97 also created a new temporary "family credit" for non-child credit eligible dependents (children ineligible for the child tax credit or older non-child dependents). Non-child credit eligible dependents excludes otherwise eligible dependents who are citizens of Mexico or Canada. The credit is equal to $500 per non-child credit eligible dependent. The amount is not annually adjusted for inflation. The phaseout parameters of the child credit (i.e., phaseout thresholds of $400,000 married filing jointly, $200,000 other taxpayers, 5% phaseout rate) apply to the family credit. The family credit is not annually adjusted for inflation.

All the modifications to the child tax credit and the new family credit are currently scheduled to expire at the end of 2025.

Chapter 4 - Beginning in the late 1970s, highly publicized cases of children who were abducted, sexually abused, and sometimes murdered prompted policymakers and child advocates to declare a missing children problem. At that time, about 1.8 million children annually were reported to the police as missing. More recent data indicate that the number and rate at which children go missing has declined. A survey from 2013 provides the most recent and comprehensive information on missing children. The data show that about 238,000 children (3.1 per 1,000 children) were reported to law enforcement by their caretakers that year as missing due to a family or nonfamily abduction; running away or being forced to leave home; becoming lost or injured; or for benign reasons, such as a miscommunication about schedules.

As a policy issue, missing children are often included in discussions of sexual victimization. Children who go missing—as well as children who are not missing—may be sexually exploited. A study that examined the prevalence of children's exposure to violence in 2008 found that 1 in 16 (6.1%) surveyed children were sexually victimized in the past year and nearly 1 in 10 (9.8%) were sexually victimized at some point over their lifetimes.

Recognizing the need for greater federal coordination of local and state efforts to recover missing and exploited children, Congress passed the Missing Children's Assistance Act (P.L. 98-473) in 1984. The act directed the U.S. Department of Justice's (DOJ's) Office of Juvenile Justice and Delinquency Prevention (OJJDP) to establish a national resource center for missing and exploited children, among other related activities. The Missing Children's Assistance Act has been amended multiple times, most recently in 2013 (P.L. 113-38).

Activities authorized under the Missing Children's Assistance Act and selected other laws are collectively referred to as the Missing and Exploited Children's (MEC) program. The program includes the following components:

- The National Center for Missing and Exploited Children (NCMEC): Since 1984, NCMEC has served as the national resource center and has carried out many of the objectives of the Missing Children's Assistance Act in collaboration with OJJDP.
- The Internet Crimes Against Children (ICAC) Task Force program: This program assists state and local enforcement cyber units in investigating online child sexual exploitation. It was authorized under the PROTECT Our Children Act of 2008 (P.L. 110-401), as amended.
- Training and technical assistance for state AMBER (America's Missing: Broadcast Emergency Response) Alert systems: AMBER Alerts publicly broadcast bulletins in the most serious child abduction cases. The AMBER Alert program is authorized under the PROTECT Act (P.L. 108-21).
- Other initiatives: These include training and technical assistance on investigating and preventing child victimization. They also include support to membership-based nonprofit missing and exploited children's organizations. These initiatives are authorized by the Missing Children's Assistance Act.

FY2017 appropriations to DOJ for the MEC program were $72.5 million, of which $28.3 million was for NCMEC, $27.6 million was for the ICAC Task Force program, $2.4 million was for the AMBER Alert program, and $4.2 million was for other initiatives. The remaining amount was allocated for other DOJ activities.

Chapter 5 - On September 5, 2017, Attorney General Jeff Sessions announced that the Deferred Action for Childhood Arrivals (DACA) policy, an Obama Administration initiative, was being rescinded. A related memorandum released by the Department of Homeland Security (DHS) that same day rescinded the 2012 memorandum that established DACA and described how DHS would "execute a wind-down of the program." According to the September 2017 memorandum, DHS will continue to adjudicate certain DACA requests and will not terminate previously issued grants of deferred action or employment authorization "solely based on the directives in this memorandum."

DACA was established in June 2012, when DHS announced that certain individuals without a lawful immigration status who were brought to the United States as children and met other criteria would be considered for temporary relief from removal. To request DACA (initial or renewal), an individual has to file specified forms with DHS's U.S. Citizenship and Immigration Services (USCIS) and pay associated fees. USCIS's decision on an initial DACA request or a renewal request is discretionary. DACA recipients are not granted a lawful immigration status and are not put on a pathway to a lawful immigration status. They are, however, considered to be lawfully present in the United States during the period of deferred action.

Cumulatively, through March 31, 2017, USCIS approved 787,580 initial DACA requests and 799,077 renewal requests. The overall approval rates for DACA requests accepted and decided by March 31, 2017, were approximately 92% for initial requests and 99% for renewals.

To date, Congress has considered, but never enacted, legislation on the DACA initiative. Several bills introduced in the 115th Congress would provide different forms of immigration protection to unauthorized childhood arrivals who satisfy specified eligibility criteria. Some of these bills would provide temporary protection from removal and employment authorization to eligible individuals, while other measures would establish pathways for eligible individuals to become U.S. lawful permanent residents (LPRs).

This report provides answers to frequently asked questions about the DACA initiative.

In: Children's Issues and Legislation ISBN: 978-1-53614-493-2
Editor: Christie Nguyen

Chapter 1

RUNAWAY AND HOMELESS YOUTH: DEMOGRAPHICS AND PROGRAMS (UPDATED)*

Adrienne L. Fernandes-Alcantara

SUMMARY

This report discusses runaway and homeless youth, and the federal response to support this population. There is no single definition of the terms "runaway youth" or "homeless youth." However, both groups of youth share the risk of not having adequate shelter and other provisions, and may engage in harmful behaviors while away from a permanent home. These two groups also include "thrownaway" youth who are asked to leave their homes, and may include other vulnerable youth populations, such as current and former foster youth and youth with mental health or other issues. The term "unaccompanied youth" encompasses both runaways and homeless youth, and is used in national data counts of the population.

* This is an edited, reformatted and augmented version of Congressional Research Service, Publication No. RL33785, dated April 26, 2018.

Youth most often cite family conflict as the major reason for their homelessness or episodes of running away. A youth's sexual orientation, sexual activity, school problems, and substance abuse are associated with family discord. The precise number of homeless and runaway youth is unknown due to their residential mobility and overlap among the populations. Determining the number of these youth is further complicated by the lack of a standardized methodology for counting the population and inconsistent definitions of what it means to be homeless or a runaway. According to a federally funded study, over 4 million youth ages 13 through 25 experienced a form of homelessness over a 12-month period.

From the early 20th century through the 1960s, the needs of runaway and homeless youth were handled locally through the child welfare agency, juvenile justice courts, or both. The 1970s marked a shift toward federal oversight of programs that help youth who had run afoul of the law, including those who committed status offenses (e.g., running away). Congress and the President enacted the Runaway Youth Act of 1974 as Title III of the Juvenile Justice and Delinquency Prevention Act (P.L. 93-415) to assist runaways through services specifically for this population. These services are provided through the federal Runaway and Homeless Youth Program. The program has been updated through reauthorization laws, most recently by the Reconnecting Homeless Youth Act (P.L. 110-378) in 2008. The program is funded through the annual appropriations process. The authorization of appropriations expired in FY2013. Congress and the President have continued to provide funds for the act: $127.4 million was appropriated for FY2018.

The Runaway and Homeless Youth program is made up of three components: the Basic Center Program (BCP), Transitional Living Program (TLP), and Street Outreach Program (SOP). The Basic Center Program provides temporary shelter, counseling, and after care services to runaway and homeless youth under age 18 and their families. The BCP has served approximately 31,000 youth annually in recent years. The Transitional Living Program is targeted to older youth ages 16 through 22 (and sometimes an older age), and has served approximately 6,000 annually in recent years. Youth who use the TLP receive longer-term housing with supportive services. The SOP provides education, treatment, counseling, and referrals for runaway, homeless, and street youth who have been subjected to or are at risk of being subjected to sexual abuse, sex exploitation, and trafficking. The SOP makes contact with about 36,000 street youth annually.

Related services authorized by the Runaway and Homeless Youth Act include a national communication system to facilitate communication between service providers, runaway youth, and their families; training and technical support for grantees; and evaluations of the programs, among other activities. The 2008 reauthorization expanded the program, requiring HHS to conduct an incidence and prevalence study of runaway and homeless youth. Congress and the President provided appropriations to the U.S. Department of Housing and Urban Development (HUD) for the study, and initial findings were published in 2017. Additional efforts are underway among multiple federal agencies to collect better information on these youth as part of a larger strategy to end youth homelessness by 2020. In addition to the Runaway and Homeless Youth Program, other federal programs support runaway and homeless youth.

INTRODUCTION

Running away from home is not a recent phenomenon. Folkloric heroes Huckleberry Finn and Davy Crockett fled their abusive fathers to find adventure and employment. Although some youth today also leave home due to abuse and neglect, they often endure far more negative outcomes than their romanticized counterparts from an earlier era. Without adequate and safe shelter, runaway and homeless youth are vulnerable to engaging in high-risk behaviors and further victimization. Youth who live away from home for extended periods may become removed from school and systems of support that promote positive development. Runaway and homeless youth are vulnerable to multiple problems while they are away from a permanent home, including untreated mental health disorders, drug use, and sexual exploitation. They also report other challenges including poor health and the lack of basic provisions.[1]

Congress began to hear concerns about the vulnerabilities of the runaway population in the 1970s due to increased awareness about these youth and the establishment of runaway shelters to assist them in returning home. Congress and the President went on to enact the

---

[1] Paul A.Toro, Amy Dworsky, and Patrick J. Fowler, *Homeless Youth in the United States: Recent Research Findings and Intervention Approaches*, HUD, Office of Policy Development and Research, September 2007, https://www.huduser.gov/portal/publications/homeless/p6.html. (Hereinafter, Paul A.Toro, Amy Dworsky, and Patrick J. Fowler,*Homeless Youth in the United States: Recent Research Findings and Intervention Approaches*.)

Runaway Youth Act of 1974 as Title III of the Juvenile Justice and Delinquency Prevention Act (P.L. 93-415) to assist runaways through services specifically for this population. Since that time, the law has been updated to authorize services to provide support for runaway and homeless youth outside of the juvenile justice, mental health, and child welfare systems. The Runaway Youth Act—now known as the Runaway and Homeless Youth Act—authorized federal funding to be provided through annual appropriations for three programs to assist runaway and homeless youth—the Basic Center Program (BCP), Transitional Living Program (TLP), and Street Outreach Program (SOP)—through FY2013.[2] Congress and the President have continued to appropriate funding for the three programs. Together, the programs make up the Runaway and Homeless Youth Program (RHYP), administered by the Family and Youth Services Bureau (FYSB) in the U.S. Department of Health and Human Services' (HHS) Administration for Children and Families (ACF).

- ***Basic Center Program:*** Provides crisis intervention, temporary shelter, counseling, family unification, and after care services to runaway and homeless youth under age 18 and their families. In some cases, BCP-funded programs may serve older youth. The program served over 31,000 youth in FY2016.
- ***Transitional Living Program:*** Supports projects that provide homeless youth ages 16 through 22 with stable, safe longer-term residential services up to 18 months (or longer under

[2] The Runaway and Homeless Youth Act was most recently reauthorized by the Runaway and Homeless Youth Protection Act (P.L. 110-378). For additional information about the 2008 reauthorization law, see CRS Report RL34483, *Runaway and Homeless Youth: Reauthorization Legislation and Issues in the 110th Congress*. The law is authorized at 34 U.S.C. §10101 et seq.: Basic Center Program (34 U.S.C. §§11211-11213), Transitional Living Program (34 U.S.C. §§11221 – 11222), and Street Outreach Program (34 U.S.C. §11261). The law refers to the SOP as the Sexual Abuse Prevention program. Accompanying regulations are at 45 C.F.R. §1351 et seq. Information about these program is drawn from statute, congressional budget justifications, reports to Congress, and funding announcements.

certain circumstances), including counseling in basic life skills, building interpersonal skills, educational advancement, job attainment skills, and physical and mental health care. The program served over 6,000 youth in FY2016.

- ***Street Outreach Program:*** Provides street-based outreach and education, including treatment, counseling, provision of information, and referrals for runaway, homeless, and street youth who have been subjected to or are at risk of being subjected to sexual abuse, sexual exploitation, prostitution, and trafficking. SOP grantees made contact with more than 36,000 youth in FY2016.

This report begins with an overview of the runaway and homeless youth population.[3] The report then describes the challenges in defining and counting the runaway and homeless youth population, as well as the factors that influence homelessness and leaving home. The report also provides background on the evolution of the Runaway and Homeless Youth Act from the 1970s until it was last amended in 2008. It then describes the administration and funding of the Basic Center, Transitional Living, and Street Outreach programs that were created from authorizations in the act. Finally, the report discusses other federal programs that may be used to assist runaway and homeless youth.

WHO ARE HOMELESS AND RUNAWAY YOUTH?

Defining the Population

There is no single federal definition of the terms "homeless youth" or "runaway youth." However, HHS relies on the various definitions

---

[3] For information about reauthorization, see CRS Report R43766, *Runaway and Homeless Youth Act: Current Issues for Reauthorization*.

from the program's authorizing legislation and its accompanying regulations. The Runaway and Homeless Youth Act defines homeless youth for purposes of the BCP as individuals under age 18 (or some older age if permitted by state or local law) for whom it is not possible to live in a safe environment with a relative and lack safe alternative living arrangements. For purposes of the TLP, homeless youth are individuals ages 16 through 22 for whom it is not possible to live in a safe environment with a relative and lack safe alternative living arrangements. Youth older than age 22 may participate if they entered the program before age 22 and meet other requirements. The act describes runaway youth as individuals under age 18 who absent themselves from their home or legal residence at least overnight without the permission of their parents or legal guardians.

Separately, the McKinney-Vento Act authorizes several federal programs for homeless individuals that are administered by the U.S. Department of Housing and Urban Development (HUD). The definition of "homeless individual" in McKinney-Vento includes "unaccompanied youth," which applies to selected homelessness programs. The regulation defines an "unaccompanied youth" as someone under age 25 who meets the definition of "homeless" in the Runaway and Homeless Youth or other specified federal laws.[4] The regulation also provides additional criteria, including that they have experienced at least 60 days of living independently without permanent housing.[5]

The research literature also includes definitions of runaway and homeless youth may include a sub-population known as "thrownaway" youth (or "push outs") who have been abandoned by their parents or

---

[4] These other programs are not focused on youth per se. The act also authorizes the Education for Homeless Children and Youths program, which is administered by the U.S. Department of Education (ED) and provides supports to assist homeless children and unaccompanied youth in schools. The program defines homelessness in part by reference to the definition of "homeless individual," as well as other criteria. For some of these definitions, see CRS Report RL30442, *Homelessness: Targeted Federal Programs.*

[5] U.S. Department of Housing and Urban Development, "Homeless Emergency Assistance and Rapid Transition to Housing: Defining 'Homeless'," 76 *Federal Register* 75994-76019, December 5, 2011.

have been told to leave their households. While studies have often categorized young people based on their status as *runaways, thrownaways, or street youth*, a 2011 report suggests that overlap exists between these categories. The authors of the study note that these "typologies," or classifications, are too narrowly defined by the youth's housing status and reasons for homelessness, among other factors. The authors explain that typologies based on mental health status or age cohort are promising, but they suggest further research in this area to ensure that the typologies are accurate.[6]

Demographics

The precise number of homeless and runaway youth is unknown due to their residential mobility. These youth often eschew the shelter system for locations or areas that are not easily accessible to shelter workers and others who count the homeless and runaways.[7] Youth who come into contact with census takers may also be reluctant to report that they have left home or are homeless. Determining the number of homeless and runaway youth is further complicated by the lack of a standardized methodology for counting the population and inconsistent definitions of what it means to be homeless or a runaway.[8] Further, some studies examine homelessness based on the age of youth (e.g., under age 18, or 18 and older).

Differences in methodology for collecting data on homeless populations may also influence how the characteristics of the runaway and homeless youth population are reported. Some studies have relied

---

[6] Paul A. Toro, Tegan M. Lesperance, and Jordan M. Braciszewski, *The Heterogeneity of Homeless Youth in America: Examining Typologies*, Homeless Research Institute, September 2011, pp. 1-12.

[7] Christopher L. Ringwalt et al., "The Prevalence of Homelessness Among Adolescents in the United States," *American Journal of Public Health*, vol. 88, no. 9 (September 1998), p. 1325 (hereinafter, Christopher L. Ringwalt et al., "The Prevalence of Homelessness Among Adolescents").

[8] Ibid.

on point prevalence estimates that report whether youth have experienced homelessness at a given point in time, such as on a particular day.[9] According to researchers that study the characteristics of runaway and homeless youth, these studies appear to be biased toward describing individuals who experience longer periods of homelessness.[10] The sample location may also misrepresent the characteristics of the population generally.[11] Youth surveyed in locations with high rates of drug use and sex work, known as "cruise areas," tend to be older, to have been away from home longer, to have recently visited community-based agencies, and to be less likely to attend school than youth in "non-cruise areas."[12]

Further, the research literature on the number and characteristics of runaway and homeless youth is fairly limited and dated. Some of the studies focus on the demographics of either homeless youth; runaway youth; or unaccompanied youth, who can encompass both runaways and homeless youth. HUD requires communities receiving certain HUD funding to conduct annual point-in-time (PIT) counts of people experiencing homelessness, including homeless youth. In 2017, nearly 41,000 unaccompanied youth under age 25 (4,789 under age 18 and 36,010 ages 18 to 25) were identified in the PIT count. Another 9,436 youth under age 25 were homeless parents.[13] While PIT counts do not provide a confident estimate of youth experiencing homelessness across the country, they provide some information to communities about the potential scope of youth homelessness.[14]

---

[9] Ibid.

[10] Ibid.

[11] Andrea L. Witkin et al., "Finding Homeless Youth: Patterns Based on Geographical Area and Number of Homeless Episodes," *Youth & Society*, vol. 37, no. 1 (September 2005), pp. 62-63.

[12] Ibid.

[13] U.S. Department of Housing and Urban Development (HUD), *HUD 2017 Continuum of Care Homeless Assistance Programs Populations and Subpopulations,* 2017, https://www.hudexchange.info/resource/ reportmanagement/published/CoC_PopSub_NatlTerrDC_2017.pdf.

[14] U.S. Interagency Council on Homelessness (USICH), *Framework to End Youth Homelessness: A Resource Text for Dialogue and Action*, February 2013, p. 4, (hereinafter, *Framework to*

The Reconnecting Homeless Youth Act (P.L. 110-378), which renewed authorization of appropriations for the Runaway and Homeless Youth Program through FY2013, also authorized funding for HHS to conduct periodic studies of the incidence and prevalence of youth who have run away or are homeless. The accompanying conference report to the FY2016 appropriations law (P.L. 114-113) directed HUD to use $2 million to conduct a national incidence and prevalence study of homeless youth as authorized under the Runaway and Homeless Youth program. HUD provided these funds to Chapin Hall at the University of Chicago to carry out the study.[15]

The study, *Voices of Youth Count*, used a nationally representative phone survey for national estimates and conducted brief surveys of youth and in-depth interviews of youth who had experiences of homelessness. The study interviewed adults whose households had youth and young adults ages 13 to 25 and respondents ages 18 to 25. *Voices of Youth Count* found that approximately 700,000 youth ages 13 to 17 and 3.5 million young adults ages 18 to 25 had experienced homelessness within a one-year period. The study also found that youth homelessness affects youth in rural and urban areas at similar levels.[16]

Factors Influencing Homelessness and Leaving Home

Youth most often cite family conflict as the major reason for their homelessness or episodes of running away. A literature review of

---

End Youth Homelessness: A Resource Text for Dialogue and Action.) USICH, HUD, *Point-in-Time Count Methodology Guide,* 2014, p. 61.

[15] HUD, Office of Policy Development and Research, *PD&R Edge Online Magazine*, "HUD Funding Supports Chapin Hall's *Voices of Youth* Enabling Collection of Crucial Data on Youth Homelessness," August 2016, https://www.huduser.gov/portal/pdredge/pdr-edge-frm-asst-sec-080816.html.

[16] Matthew H. Morton, Amy Dworsky, and Gina M. Samuels, *Missed Opportunities: Youth Homelessness in America. National Estimates*, University of Chicago, Chapin Hall, 2017. (Hereinafter, Matthew H. Morton, Amy Dworsky, and Gina M. Samuels, *Missed Opportunities: Youth Homelessness in America. National Estimates*).

homeless youth found that a youth's relationship with a stepparent, sexual activity, sexual orientation, pregnancy, school problems, and alcohol and drug use were strong predictors of family discord.[17] Over one-third of callers who used the National Runaway Safeline in 2016—a federally sponsored call center funded under the Runaway and Homeless Youth Program for youth and their relatives involved in runaway incidents—gave family dynamics (not defined) as the reason for their call.[18] Further, a longitudinal survey of middle school and high school youth examined the effects of family instability (e.g., child maltreatment, lack of parental warmth, and parent rejection) and other factors on the likelihood of running away from home approximately two to six years after youth were initially surveyed.

Researchers found that youth with family instability were more likely to run away. Family instability also influenced problem behaviors, such as illicit drug use, which, in turn, were associated with running away. Running away also increased the chances of running again. Researchers further determined that environmental effects (e.g., school engagement, neighborhood cohesiveness, physical victimization, and friends' support) were not strong predicators of whether youth in the sample ran away.[19]

The *Voices of Youth Count* study found that certain youth ages 18 to 25 were at heightened risk of experiencing homelessness, including those with less than a high school diploma or GED; who are Hispanic or black; who are parenting and unmarried; or who are lesbian, gay, bisexual, transgender, or questioning (LGBTQ).[20] Gay and lesbian

[17] Paul A.Toro, Amy Dworsky, and Patrick J. Fowler, *Homeless Youth in the United States: Recent Research Findings and Intervention Approaches.*

[18] National Runaway Safeline, "Crisis Hotline & Online Service Statistics," http://www.1800runaway.org/runawaystatistics/crisis-hotline-online-services-statistics/.

[19] Kimberly A. Tyler, Kellie J. Hagewen, and Lisa A. Melander, "Risk Factors for Running Away Among a Sample of Males and Females," *Youth & Society*, vol. 43, no. 2, 2011, pp. 583-608.

[20] Matthew H. Morton, Amy Dworsky, and Gina M. Samuels, *Missed Opportunities: Youth Homelessness in America. National Estimates.*

youth appear to be at greater risk for homelessness and are overrepresented in the homeless population, due often to experiencing negative reactions from their parents when they come out about their sexuality. The *Voices of Youth Count* study found that LGBTQ young adults ages 18 to 25 had more than twice the risk of being homeless than their heterosexual peers. Further, LGBTQ youth made up about 20% of young adults who reported homelessness.[21] In addition, a nationwide survey of 354 organizations serving homeless youth in 2011 and 2012 found that LGBT youth make up about 40% of their clients.[22]

Runaway and homeless youth have described abuse and neglect as common experiences. Another study of youth who ran away from foster care between 1993 and 2003 by Chapin Hall at the University of Chicago found that the average likelihood of an individual running away from foster care placements increased over this time period.[23] Youth questioned about their runaway experiences cited three primary reasons why they ran from foster care: to connect with their biological families; express their autonomy and find normalcy; and maintain relationships with non-family members. Youth who experience foster care are also vulnerable to homelessness after emancipating from the child welfare system. In a study of 26-year-olds who had emancipated from foster care in three states, approximately 15% had experienced homelessness since their last interview at age 23; slightly over half

---

[21] Matthew H. Morton et al., *Missed Opportunities: LGBTQ Youth Homelessness in America*, University of Chicago, Chapin Hall, 2018.

[22] Laura E. Durso and Gary J. Gates, "Serving Our Youth: Findings from a National Survey of Service Providers Working with Lesbian, Gay, Bisexual, and Transgender Youth who are Homeless or At Risk of Becoming Homeless," The Williams Institute with True Colors Fund and The Palette Fund, 2012, https://williamsinstitute.law.ucla.edu/research/safe-schools-and-youth/serving-our-youth-july-2012/. https://www.hudexchange.info/resource/reportmanagement/published/CoC_PopSub_NatlTerrDC_2017.pdf.

[23] Mark E. Courtney et al., "Youth Who Run Away from Out-of-Home Care," *Chapin Hall Center for Children Issue Brief*, no. 103 (March 2005), p. 2, http://www.chapinhall.org/research/brief/youth-who-run-away-out-home-care.

stated that they had been homeless more than once, and almost one-quarter stated they had been homeless four or more times.[24]

EVOLUTION OF FEDERAL POLICY

Prior to the enactment of the Runaway Youth Act of 1974 (Title III, Juvenile Justice and Delinquency Prevention Act of 1974, P.L. 93-415), federal policy provided limited services to runaway and homeless youth. If they received any services, most of these youth were served through the local child welfare agency, juvenile justice court system, or both. The 1970s marked a shift to a more rehabilitative model for assisting youth who had run afoul of the law, including those who committed status offenses such as running away. During this period, Congress focused increasing attention on runaways and other vulnerable youth due, in part, to emerging sociological models to explain why youth engaged in deviant behavior. The first runaway shelters were created in the late 1960s and 1970s to assist them in returning home. The landmark Runaway Youth Act of 1974 decriminalized runaway youth and authorized funding for programs to provide shelter, counseling, and other services. Since the law's enactment, Congress and the President have expanded the services available to both runaway youth and homeless youth under what is now referred to as the Runaway and Homeless Youth Program. In more recent years, other federal entities have been involved in responding to the challenges facing runaway and homeless youth. Figure 1 traces the evolution of federal policy in this area.

---

[24] Mark E. Courtney et al., *Midwest Evaluation of the Adult Functioning of Former Foster Youth: Outcomes at Age 26*, Chapin Hall Center for Children, University of Chicago, December 2011, p. 12, http://www.chapinhall.org/sites/ default/files/Midwest%20Evaluation_Report_12_30_11.pdf.

U.S. Interagency Council on Homelessness: *Opening Doors*

The Runaway and Homeless Youth Program is a major part of recent federal efforts to end youth homelessness through the U.S. Interagency Council on Homelessness (USICH). The USICH, established under the 1987 Stewart B. McKinney Homeless Assistance Act, is made up of several federal agencies, including HHS and HUD The HEARTH Act, enacted in 2009 as part of the Helping Families Save Their Homes Act (P.L. 111-22), charged USICH with developing a National Strategic Plan to End Homelessness.[25] In June 2010, USICH released this plan, entitled *Opening Doors*.[26] The plan sets out goals for ending homelessness, including (1) ending chronic homelessness by 2015; (2) preventing and ending homelessness among veterans by 2015; (3) preventing and ending homelessness for families, youth, and children by 2020; and (4) setting a path to ending all types of homelessness. In 2012, USICH amended *Opening Doors* to specifically address strategies for improving the educational outcomes for children and youth and assisting unaccompanied homeless youth.[27] USICH ultimately intends to improve outcomes for youth in four areas: stable housing, permanent connections, education or employment options, and socio-emotional well-being.

---

[25] The HEARTH Act specified that the plan should be made available for public comment and submitted to Congress and the President within one year of the law's enactment. USICH convened working groups made up of members of federal agencies to discuss ending homelessness among specific populations: families, youth, persons experiencing chronic homelessness, and veterans. USICH, *Federal Strategic Plan to Prevent and End Homelessness Overview*. The council then held regional meetings to get feedback from various stakeholders, and it accepted public comments on its website during March 2010. For public comments, see http://fsp.uservoice.com/forums/41991-how-can-the-local-community-contribute-to-the-visi.

[26] U.S. Interagency Council on Homelessness (USICH), *Opening Doors: Federal Strategic Plan to Prevent and End Homelessness*, June 2010.

[27] USICH, *Opening Doors: Federal Strategic Plan to Prevent and End Homelessness Amendment 2012*, September 2012, http://usich.gov/opening_doors/amendment_2012. See also, U.S. Interagency Council on Homelessness, Council Meeting, presentation by Bryan Samuels, Commissioner, Administration on Children, Youth and Families, June 12, 2012. Unaccompanied youth includes those on their own, youth who are parents and their children, adolescent siblings, and other groups composed of only youth.

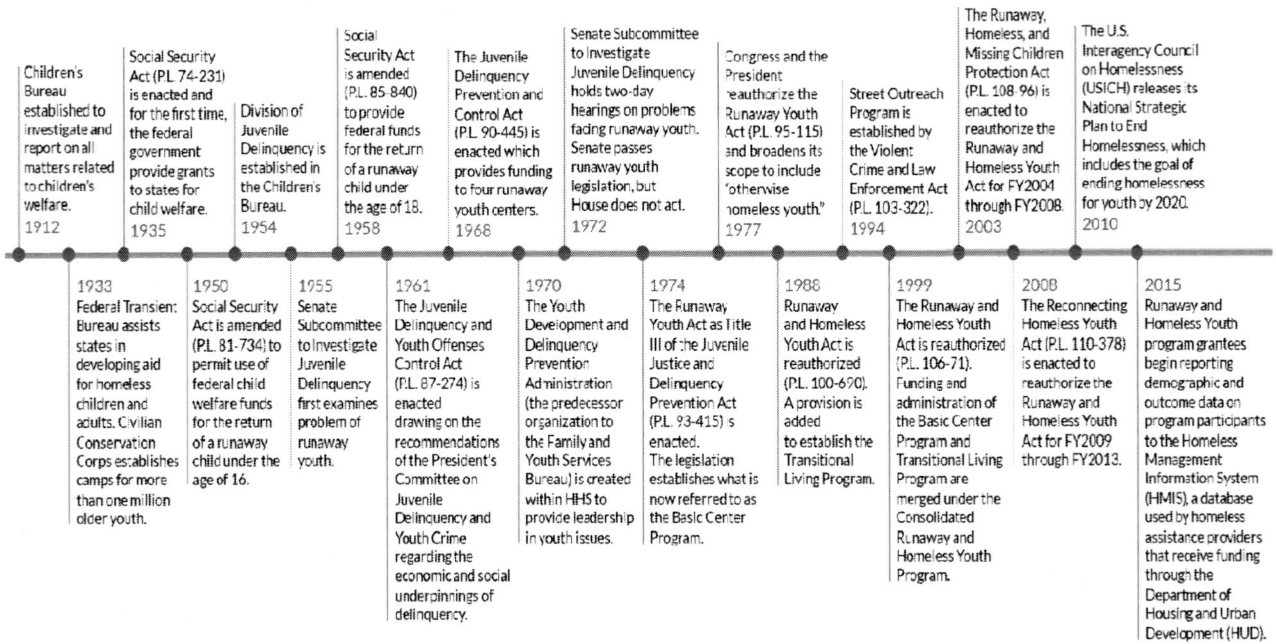

Source: Congressional Research Service (CRS).

Figure 1. Evolution of Federal Runaway and Homeless Youth Policy.

In 2013, a USICH working group developed a guiding document for ending youth homelessness by 2020. Known as the *Framework to End Youth Homelessness*, the document outlines a data strategy to collect better data on the number and characteristics of youth experiencing homelessness. This data strategy includes coordinating the data collection system for the Runaway and Homeless Youth program—referred to as RHYMIS—with HUD's Homeless Management Information Systems (HMIS). RHYMIS was a data system administered by HHS for previous RHYP grantees to upload demographic and other data for the youth they served. HMIS is a locally administered data system used to record and analyze client, service, and housing data for individuals and families who are homeless or at risk of homelessness in a given community.[28]

As of FY2015, RHYP grantees stopped reporting to RHYMIS and instead report to HMIS. Grantees reported to RHYMIS on the basic demographics of the youth, the services they received, and the status of the youth upon exiting the programs. RHY grantees are now required to report this same (and new information) to HMIS. The data strategy outlined in the framework also involves, if funding is available, designing and implementing a national study to estimate the number, needs, and characteristics of youth experiencing homelessness. This is consistent with the Runaway and Homeless Youth Act's directive for HHS to conduct a study of youth homelessness. As noted, this study was first conducted with funding from HUD.

Separately, the framework's capacity strategy seeks to strengthen and coordinate the capacity of federal, state, and local systems to work toward ending youth homelessness. USICH has provided guidance to communities, including by establishing community-level criteria for

---

[28] HUD, *2014 HMIS Data Standards: HMIS Data Dictionary*, version 2.1, August 2014, and *2014 HMIS Data Standards Manual: A Guide for HMIS Users, CoCs and System Administrators*, version 2.1, August 2014, https://www.hudexchange.info/hmis/hmis-regulations-and-notices.

ending homelessness and accompanying benchmarks to assess whether they have achieved an end to youth homelessness.[29]

RUNAWAY AND HOMELESS YOUTH PROGRAM

Federal Administration and Funding

As mentioned, the Runaway and Homeless Youth Program is administered by the Family and Youth Services Bureau (FYSB) within HHS's Administration for Children and Families (ACF). The funding streams for the Basic Center Program and Transitional Living Program were separate until they were consolidated as part of reauthorization of the Runaway and Homeless Youth Act in 1999 (P.L. 106-71). Under current law, 90% of the federal funds appropriated under the consolidated program must be used for the BCP and TLP (together, the programs and their related activities are known as the Consolidated Runaway and Homeless Youth program). Of this amount, 45% is reserved for the BCP and no more than 55% is reserved for the TLP. The remaining share of federal funding is allocated for (1) a national communication system to facilitate communication between service providers, runaway youth, and their families; (2) training and technical support for grantees; (3) evaluations of the programs; (4) federal coordination efforts on matters relating to the health, education, employment, and housing of these youth; and (5) studies of runaway and homeless youth. The Street Outreach program is funded separately from the BCP and TLP. Although the SOP is a separately funded component, SOP services are coordinated with those provided under the BCP and TLP.

---

[29] USICH, *Framework to End Youth Homelessness: A Resource Text for Dialogue and Action*; USICH, *Preventing and Ending Youth Homelessness: A Coordinated Community Response*, 2015; USICH, *Ending Youth Homelessness Guidebooks*, August 2016; USICH, *Criteria and Benchmarks for Achieving the Goal of Ending Youth Homelessness*, January 2017; and USICH, *Advancing an End to Youth Homelessness: Federal and National Initiatives*, July 2017.

Table 1 shows funding levels for the Runaway and Homeless Youth Program from FY2002 through FY2018.[30] Over this period, funding has notably increased for the program four times— from FY2001 to FY2002; FY2007 to FY2008; FY2015 to FY2016; and FY2017 to FY2018. The first increase was due to the doubling of funding for the Transitional Living Program. Although the TLP authorized services for pregnant and parenting teens prior to FY2002, the Bush Administration sought funds specifically to serve this population and the increased funds were ultimately provided to enable these youth to access TLP services. In FY2003, amendments to the Runaway and Homeless Youth Act (P.L. 108-96) authorized TLP funds to be used for services targeted at pregnant and parenting teens at TLP centers known as Maternity Group Homes. The second funding increase was likely due in part to heightened attention to the RHYP, as Congress began to consider legislation in FY2008 to reauthorize the program.

Subsequent funding increases have included the change in BCP and TLP funding from FY2015 ($114.1 million) to FY2016 ($119.1 million) and again from FY2017 ($119.1 million) to FY2018 ($127.4 million). Increases since FY2015 appear to have been made possible because of the overall increase in discretionary spending limits as part of budget deals over this period.[31] Congress has provided some guidance on how the additional funds are to be spent. In the accompanying explanatory statement to accompany the FY2018 consolidated appropriations act, Congress stated that the increase should be provided to current TLP grantees whose awards end on April 30, 2018. The funding is to be used to continue services until new awards are made to those grantees, or for those grantees that did not receive a new grant, to provide services until the end of FY2018. Funding may be used for additional new awards after funds have been

---

[30] The program did not receive funding under the American Recovery and Reinvestment Act of 2009 (P.L. 110-5), the omnibus stimulus law

[31] For further information, see CRS Report R44874, *The Budget Control Act: Frequently Asked Questions*.

set aside to ensure that current grantees are able to operate through the end of FY2018.[32]

Basic Center Program

Overview

The Basic Center Program is intended to provide short-term shelter and services for youth and their families through public and private community-based centers. Youth eligible to receive BCP services include those youth who are at risk of running away or becoming homeless (and may live at home with their parents), or have already left home, either voluntarily or involuntarily. To stay at the shelter, youth must be under age 18, or an older age if the BCP center is located in a state or locality that permits this higher age. Some centers may serve homeless youth through street-based services, home-based services, and drug abuse education and prevention services.

As specified in the law, BCP centers are intended to provide these services as an alternative to involving runaway and homeless youth in the law enforcement, juvenile justice, child welfare, and mental health systems. In FY2016, the program provided services to 31,286 youth at 280 BCP shelters in all 50 states, the District of Columbia, American Samoa, Guam, and Puerto Rico.[33] These centers, which can shelter as many as 20 youth, are generally supposed to be located in areas that are frequented or easily reached by runaway and homeless youth. The shelters seek to connect youth with their families, whenever possible, or to locate appropriate alternative placements. They also provide food, clothing, individual or group and family counseling, mentoring, and

---

[32] U.S. House of Representatives, *Congressional Record*, vol. 164, part No. 50, Book III (March 22, 2018), p. H2704.

[33] HHS, ACF, *Justification of Estimates for Appropriations Committees, FY2019*, p. 134. RHY program providers began reporting data on youth in their programs to HUD and HHS via the Homeless Management Information System (HMIS) in FY2015.

Table 1. Runaway and Homeless Youth Program Funding, FY2005-FY2018 (as enacted) (Dollars in thousands)

Program	2005	2006	2007[a]	2008[b]	2009	2010	2011[c]	2012[d]	2013[e]	2014	2015	2016	2017	2018
BCP	$48,786	$48,265	$48,298	$52,860	$53,469	$53,744	$53,637	$53,536	$50,097	$53,350	$53,350	$54,439	$48.236	$110,280[f]
TLPg	39,938	39,511	39,539	43,268	43,765	43,990	43,902	43,819	41,004	43,650	43,650	47,541	53,744	
SOP	15,178	15,017	15,027	17,221	17,721	17,971	17,935	17,901	16,751	17,141	17,141	17,141	17,141	17,141
Total	103,902	102,793	102,864	113,349	114,955	115,705	115,474	115,256	107,852	114,141	114,141	119,121	119,121	127,421

Source: U.S. Department of Health and Human Services (HHS), Administration for Children and Families (ACF) *Justification of Estimates for Appropriations Committees, FY2003*, p. H-48 (hereinafter, HHS, *ACF Justification*); HHS, *ACF Justification, FY2004*, p. H-45; HHS, *ACF Justification, FY2005*, p. H-89; HHS, *ACF Justification, FY2006*, p. D-41; HHS, *ACF Justification, FY2007*, p. D-41; HHS, *ACF Justification, FY2008*, pp. 92, 98; HHS, *ACF Justification, FY2009*, p. D-42; HHS, *ACF Justification FY2010*, pp. 85, 92; HHS, *ACF Justification, FY2012*, pp. 101, 109; HHS, *ACF Justification, FY2013*, pp. 106, 113; HHS, *ACF Justification, FY2014*, pp. 105, 114; U.S. HHS, ACF, *All-Purpose Table—FY2012-2013;* HHS, *ACF Justification, FY2016*; and HHS, ACF, *ACF Justification*; "FY2017 ACF Operating Plan; and CRS correspondence with HHS, Office of the Assistant Secretary for Legislation, December 2017; and U.S. House of Representatives, *Congressional Record*, vol. 164, part No. 50, Book III (March 22, 2018), p. H2744.

Notes: BCP and TLP funds are appropriated together under what is known as the Consolidated Runaway and Homeless Youth program. SOP funds are appropriated separately. Appropriation law sometimes refers to the SOP as Prevention Grants to Reduce Abuse of Runaway Youth.

[a] The fourth continuing resolution for FY2007 (P.L. 110-5) generally funded programs at their FY2006 levels. However, the FY2006 funding total for the RHYP was slightly lower than the FY2007 total because of an additional transfer of funds from the RHYP accounts to an HHS sub-agency.

[b] The FY2008 appropriations include a 1.7% across-the-board rescission on Labor-HHS-Education programs.

[c] The FY2011 appropriations include a 0.2% across-the-board rescission.

[d] The FY2012 appropriations include a 0.189% across-the-board rescission.

[e] The FY2013 appropriations include amounts provided in the final FY2013 appropriations law (P.L. 113-6), an across-the-board rescission of 0.2% required by Section 3004 of the final FY2013 appropriations law (as interpreted by the Office of Management and Budget), reductions required by the sequestration order of March 1, 2013, and any potential transfers or reprogramming of funds pursuant to the authority of the Secretary.

[f] The Consolidated Appropriations Act, 2018 (P.L. 115-141) provided funding for both the BCP and TLP under a lump sum appropriation for the "Consolidated Runaway, Homeless Youth Program." HHS is to determine the funding allocation for the BCP and TLP according to the requirements in the law.

[g] Since FY2004, the TLP has included funding for the Maternity Group Home component.

health care referrals. Youth may stay in a center continuously up to 21 days and may re-enter the program multiple times. BCP grantees—public and private nonprofit organizations—must make efforts to contact the parents and relatives of runaway and homeless youth. Grantees are also required to establish relationships with law enforcement, health and mental health care, social service, welfare, and school district systems to coordinate services. Centers maintain confidential statistical records of youth, including youth who are not referred to out-of-home shelter services, and the family members. The centers are required to submit an annual report to HHS detailing the program activities and the number of youth participating in such activities, as well as information about the operation of the centers.

Funding Allocation

BCP grants are allocated directly to nonprofit entities for three-year periods. Funding is generally distributed to entities based on the proportion of the nation's youth under age 18 in the jurisdiction (50 states, the District of Columbia, and the U.S. territories) where the entities are located. The states, the District of Columbia, and Puerto Rico[34] receive a minimum allotment of $200,000. Separately, the territories (currently, this includes American Samoa and Guam) receive a minimum of $70,000. The amount of funding for each state or territory can further depend on whether grant applicants in that jurisdiction applied for funding, and if so, whether the applicant fulfilled the requirements in the authorizing law and grant application. For example, the authorizing law directs HHS to give priority to applicants who have demonstrated experience in providing services to runaway and homeless youth. HHS is to re-allot any funds designated for grantees in one state to grantees in other states that will not be obligated before the end of a fiscal year. See the Appendix for the

[34] Puerto Rico is treated like a state and receives an annual allotment based on the populations of individuals under the age of 18 living in the territory. CRS correspondence with HHS, ACF, ACYF, FYSB, May 2016.

amount of funding allocated for each state in FY2016 and FY2017. The costs of the BCP are shared by the federal government (90%) and grantees (10%). Grants may be awarded for up to three years.

Rural Homeless Youth Demonstration

In FY2008, HHS began funding a three-year Rural Host Homes Demonstration Project, which was initiated to expand BCP shelter and support services to runaway and homeless youth who live in rural areas not served by shelter facilities. The project supported grantees that provided youth with shelter (via host home families who were recruited, screened, and trained) and preventive services including transportation, counseling, educational assistance, and aftercare planning, among others. Over the course of the three years, the project served 781 youth, 411 of whom received shelter and 370 of whom received preventive services without shelter.[35]

Transitional Living Program

Overview

Recognizing the difficulty that youth face in becoming self-sufficient adults, the Transitional Living Program provides longer-term shelter and assistance for youth ages 16 through 22 (or older if the youth entered the TLP prior to reaching age 22) who may leave their biological homes due to family conflict, or have left and are not expected to return home. Pregnant and/or parenting youth are eligible for TLP services. In FY2016, the TLP provided services to 6,054 youth at 213 organizations.[36]

---

[35] HHS, ACF, ACYF, FYSB, *Report to Congress on the Runaway and Homeless Youth Programs of the Family and Youth Services Bureau for Fiscal Years 2012 and 2013*, pp. 54-58. HHS is authorized to fund demonstration projects that address the special needs of runaway youth and homeless youth programs in rural areas and the special needs of programs that place runaway youth and homeless youth in host family homes, among other needs, under 34 U.S.C. §11244.

[36] HHS, ACF, *Justification of Estimates for Appropriations Committees, FY2019*, p. 134.

Each TLP grantee may shelter up to 20 youth at longer-term sites (e.g., host family homes, supervised apartments owned by a social service agency, scattered-site apartments, or single-occupancy apartments rented directly with the assistance of the agency). Youth may remain at TLP projects for up to 540 days (18 months), or longer for youth under age 18. Youth ages 16 through 22 may remain in the program for a continuous period of 635 days (approximately 21 months) under "exceptional circumstances." This term means circumstances in which a youth would benefit to an unusual extent from additional time in the program. A youth in a TLP who has not reached age 18 on the last day of the 635-day period may, in exceptional circumstances and if otherwise qualified for the program, remain in the program until his or her 18th birthday.

Youth receive several types of services at TLP-funded programs:

- basic life-skills training, including consumer education and instruction in budgeting and the use of credit;
- parenting skills (as appropriate);
- building interpersonal skills;
- educational advancement, such as GED courses and post-secondary courses;
- assistance in job preparation and attainment; and
- mental and physical health care services.

TLP centers develop a written plan designed to help youth transition to living independently or another appropriate living arrangement, and they refer youth to other systems that can coordinate to meet their educational, health care, and social service needs. The grantees must also submit an annual report to HHS that includes information regarding the activities carried out with funds and the number and characteristics of the homeless youth.

Maternity Group Homes

As part of the FY2002 budget request, the Bush Administration proposed a $33 million initiative to fund Maternity Group Homes—or centers that provide shelter to pregnant and parenting teens who are vulnerable to abuse and neglect—as a component of the TLP. The initiative was not funded as part of its FY2002 appropriation. However, that year Congress and the President provided $19.2 million in additional funding to the TLP to ensure that pregnant and parenting teens could access services (H.Rept. 107-376). The 2003 amendments to the Runaway and Homeless Youth Act (Pi. 108-96) provided authority to use TLP funds for Maternity Group Homes. Since FY2004, funding for adult-supervised transitional living arrangements that serve pregnant or parenting women ages 16 to 21 and their children has been awarded to organizations that receive TLP grants. These organizations provide youth with parenting skills, including child development education, family budgeting, health and nutrition, and other skills to promote family well-being.

Funding Allocation

TLP grants are distributed competitively by HHS to community-based public and private organizations throughout the country for five-year periods. Grantees must provide at least 10% of the total cost of the program.

Outcomes of Youth in the TLP

Efforts are underway at HHS to learn more about the long-term outcomes of 1,250 youth who are served by the TLP. The study seeks to describe the outcomes of youth who participate in the program and to isolate and describe promising practices and other factors that may contribute to their successes or challenges. Of particular interest to the study will be service delivery approaches, youth demographics, socio-emotional wellness, and life experiences. The study involves both a process evaluation and impact evaluation, with youth randomly assigned to the treatment (i.e., participation in the TLP) and control groups. The study seeks to address the following questions: (1) How do TLP programs operate, what types of program models are used to deliver services, and what services are delivered to homeless youth? (2) What are the long-term housing outcomes and protective factors for youth who participate in the TLP program immediately, six months, 12 months, and 18 months after exiting the program? (3) What interventions can be attributed to any positive outcomes experienced by youth who participate in the TLP? HHS expects that the final report of the evaluation will be available in 2019.[37]

Special Populations and Rural Homeless Youth Demonstration

In FY2016, HHS began the Transitional Living Program Special Population Demonstration project. This project is funding nine grantees over a two-year period that are testing approaches for serving populations that need additional support: LGBTQ runaway and homeless youth ages 16 to 21; and young adults who have left foster care after the ages of 18 to 21. Grantees are expected to provide strategies that help youth build protective factors, such as connections with schools, employment, and appropriate family members and other caring adults. A process evaluation will assess how grantees are implementing the demonstration project.[38]

HHS funded a project from FY2012 through FY2014 to build the capacity of TLPs in serving LGBTQ youth. Known as the "3/40 Blueprint: Creating the Blueprint to Reduce LGBTQ Youth Homelessness," the purpose of the grant was to develop information

---

[37] CRS correspondence with HHS, Office of the Assistant Secretary for Legislation, December 2017. See also, HHS, ACF, ACYF, FYSB, *Report to Congress on the Runaway and Homeless Youth Programs, Fiscal Years 2014 and 2015*, p. 48; and HHS, ACF, *Justification of Estimates for Appropriations Committees, FY2018*, p. 133.

[38] HHS, ACF, "Transitional Living Program Special Population Demonstration Project: LGBTQ Runaway and Homeless Youth and Young Adults Who Have Left Foster Care After Age 18," HHS-2016-ACF-ACYF-LG-1185; and HHS, ACF, FYSB, "2016 Transitional Living Program Special Population Demonstration Project Grant Awards," October 3, 2016.

about serving the LGBTQ youth population experiencing homelessness, such as through efforts to identify innovative intervention strategies, determining culturally appropriate screening and assessment tools, and better understanding the needs of LGBTQ youth served by RHY providers.[39]

In FY2009, HHS began the Support Systems for Rural Homeless Youth Demonstration Project. Six states received grants to support TLPs in rural communities in serving young adults who have few or no connections to a supportive family structure or community resources. The five-year project sought to provide services across three main areas:

- survival support, which includes housing, health care (including mental health), and substance abuse treatment and prevention;
- community, which includes community service, youth and adult partnerships, mentoring, and peer support groups; and
- education and employment, which includes high school or GED completion, postsecondary education, and job training and employment.

Annual grants of $200,000 were awarded to six states: Colorado, Iowa, Minnesota, Nebraska, Oklahoma, and Vermont. According to HHS, all of the sites engaged youth in positive development activities that included safe places for youth to go. In addition, they raised awareness about homelessness in rural areas and addressed some of the unique needs around employment, housing, and transportation. However, the sites also confirmed that there is a general lack of

---

39 HHS, ACF, FYSB, "Runaway and Homeless Youth Capacity Building for Lesbian, Gay, Bisexual, Transgender and/or Questioning Youth Populations, Grant Announcement," HHS-2013-ACF-ACYF-CX-0638. HHS, "Family and Youth Services Bureau-funded Project Paves the Way for Serving LGBTQ Homeless Youth." HHS stated that as of January 2018, no report had been published on the initiative. CRS correspondence with HHS, Office of the Assistant Secretary for Legislation, December 2017.

available housing for homeless youth and that transportation was the most critical impediment to serving these youth.[40]

Street Outreach Program

Overview

Runaway and homeless youth living on the streets or in areas that increase their risk of using drugs or being subjected to sexual abuse, prostitution, sexual exploitation, and trafficking[41] are eligible to receive services through the Street Outreach Program. The program's goal is to assist youth in transitioning to safe and appropriate living arrangements. SOP services include the following:

- treatment and counseling;
- crisis intervention;
- drug abuse and exploitation prevention and education activities;
- survival aid;
- street-based education and outreach;
- information and referrals; and
- follow-up support.

Funding Allocation

Grants are awarded for a three-year period, and grantees must provide 10% of the funds to cover the cost of the program. Applicants may apply for a grant each year of the three-year period, with the minimum grant amount in a given year being $100,000, and

---

[40] HHS, ACF, ACYF, FYSB, *Report to Congress on the Runaway and Homeless Youth Programs, Fiscal Years 2012 and 2013*, pp. 54-63.

[41] Trafficking could refer to labor or sex trafficking of children under age 18 and any youth served in the SOP. The law refers to the definition of "severe forms of trafficking in persons," as defined at 22 U.S.C. §7102(9) and "sex trafficking," as defined at 22 U.S.C. §7102(10). Trafficking could refer to labor or sex trafficking of children under age 18 and any youth served in the SOP.

the maximum $200,000. In FY2016, 103 grantees were funded. Those grantees contacted 36,126 youth.[42]

Data Collection Project

The Family and Youth Services Bureau created the Street Outreach Program Data Collection Project in 2012 to learn more about the lives and needs of homeless and runaway youth served by SOP grantees. The purpose of the project was to design services that will better meet the needs of these youth. FYSB collected information through focus groups and computer-assisted personal interviews with 656 youth (ages 14 to 21 years) served by SOP grantees in 11 cities. The project found that participants were homeless on average for nearly two years and had challenges with substance abuse, mental health, and exposure to trauma. Youth most identified that they were in need of job training or help finding a job, transportation assistance, and clothing. The top barriers to obtaining shelter were shelters being full, not knowing where to go for shelter, and lacking transportation to get to a shelter. The study researchers concluded that more emergency shelters could help prevent youth from sleeping on the street. Further, they noted that youth on the streets need more intensive case management (e.g., careful assessment and treatment planning, linkages to community resources, etc.) and more intensive interventions.[43]

Training and Technical Assistance: RHYTTAC

HHS funds the Runaway and Homeless Youth Training and Technical Assistance Center (RHYTTAC) to provide technical

---

42 HHS, ACF, *Justification of Estimates for Appropriations Committees, FY2019*, p. 141.

43 Melissa Welch et al., *Street Outreach Program Data Collection Project Overall Report 2013*, University of Nebraska-Lincoln for HHS, ACF, ACYF, FYSB, October 2014; and Les Whitbeck et al., *Street Outreach Program Data Collection Project Final Report*, April 2016.

assistance to RHYP grantees. HHS awarded a five-year cooperative agreement, from September 30, 2017, through September 29, 2020, to National Safe Place to operate RHYTTAC.[44] National Safe Place is a national youth outreach program that aims to educate young people about the dangers of running away or trying to resolve difficult, threatening situations on their own. RHYTTAC is designed to provide training and conference services to RHYP grantees that enhance and promote continuous quality improvement to services provided by RHYP grantees. Further, RHYTTAC offers resources and information through its website, tip sheets, a quarterly newsletter, toolkits, sample policies and procedures, and other resources. RHYTTAC also provides assistance to individual grantees in response to their questions or concerns, as well as concerns raised by HHS as part of the Runaway and Homeless Youth Program Monitoring System (see subsequent section).[45]

National Communication System: National Runaway Safeline

A portion of the funds for the BCP, TLP, and related activities—known collectively as the Consolidated Runaway and Homeless Youth Program—are allocated for a national communications system known as the National Runaway Safeline ("Safeline"). The Safeline is intended to help homeless and runaway youth (or youth who are contemplating running away) through counseling, referrals, and communicating with their families. Beginning with FY1974 and every year after, the Safeline, which until 2013 was called the National Runaway Switchboard, has been funded through the Basic Center Program grant or the Consolidated Runaway and Homeless Youth Program grant. The

---

[44] CRS correspondence with HHS, Office of the Assistant Secretary for Legislation, December 2017.

[45] For further information, see Runaway and Homeless Youth Training and Technical Assistance Center, "About Us," http://www.rhyttac.net/about/what-rhyttac.

Safeline is located in Chicago and operates each day to provide services to youth and their families across through the country. Services include (1) a channel through which runaway and homeless youth or their parents may leave messages; (2) 24-hour referrals to community resources, including shelter, community food banks, legal assistance, and social services agencies; and (3) crisis intervention counseling to youth.

In calendar year 2016, the Safeline handled over 33,000 contacts with youth (via phone, computer, emails, and postings), of which nearly three-quarters were from youth and 9% were from parents; the remaining callers were relatives, friends, and others.[46] Other services are also provided through the Safeline. Since 1995, the "Home Free" family reunification program has provided bus tickets for youth ages 12 to 21 to return home or to an alternative placement near their home through Home Free.[47]

Oversight

HHS Oversight

ACF evaluates each Runaway and Homeless Youth Program grant recipient through the Runaway and Homeless Youth Monitoring System. Staff from regional ACF offices and other grant recipients (known as peer reviewers) inspect the program site, conduct interviews, review case files and other agency documents, and conduct entry and exit conferences. The monitoring team then prepares a written report that identifies the strengths of the program and areas that require corrective action.[48]

---

[46] National Runaway Safeline, "Crisis Hotline & Online Service Statistics," http://www.1800runaway.org/runawaystatistics/crisis-hotline-online-services-statistics/.

[47] HHS, ACF, ACYF, FYSB, *Report to Congress on the Runaway and Homeless Youth Programs, Fiscal Years 2012 and 2013*, p. 33

[48] See HHS, ACF, ACYF, FYSB, *Onsite Review Protocol: Runaway and Homeless Youth Programs*, February 2009, http://www.acf.hhs.gov/sites/default/files/fysb/onsite-review-

The Reconnecting Homeless Youth Act of 2008 required that within one year of its enactment (October 8, 2009), HHS was to issue rules that specified performance standards for public and nonprofit entities that receive BCP, TLP, and SOP grants. In developing the regulations, HHS was to consult with stakeholders in the runaway and homeless youth policy community. The law further required that HHS integrate the performance standards into the grantmaking, monitoring, and evaluations processes for the BCP, TLP, and SOP. On April 14, 2014, HHS issued a notice of proposed rulemaking (NPRM) for the new performance standards and other requirements for the Runaway and Homeless youth program grantees.[49] On December 20, 2016, HHS implemented a final rule that was similar to the provisions in the NPRM.[50] These standards are used to monitor individual grantee performance.

Congressional Oversight

The Senate Committee on Health, Education, Labor, and Pensions (HELP) and the House Committee on Education and the Workforce have exercised jurisdiction over the Runaway and Homeless Youth Program. HHS must submit reports biennially to the committees on the status, activities, and accomplishments of program grant recipients and evaluations of the programs performed by HHS. The most recent report was submitted in January 2018, and covered FY2014 and FY2015.[51]

The 2003 reauthorization law (P.L. 108-96) of the Runaway and Homeless Youth Act required that HHS, in consultation with the U.S.

---

protocol.pdf; HHS, ACF, ACYF, FYSB, "New Rule Strengthens Runaway and Homeless Youth Programs to Better Serve Youth Experiencing Homelessness," https://www.acf.hhs.gov/sites/default/files/fysb/ fysb_rhy_rule_facts_20161220.pdf.

[49] HHS, ACF, FYSB, "Runaway and Homeless Youth; Proposed Rule," 79 *Federal Register* 71, April 14, 2014.

[50] HHS, ACF, FYSB, "Runaway and Homeless Youth; Final Rule," 81 *Federal Register* 244, December 20, 2016.

[51] HHS, ACF, ACYF, FYSB, *Report to Congress on the Runaway and Homeless Youth Programs of the Family and Youth Services Bureau for Fiscal Years 2014 and 2015*, January 4, 2018.

Interagency Council on Homelessness, submit a report to Congress on the promising strategies to end youth homelessness within two years of the reauthorization, in October 2005. The report was submitted to Congress in June 2007.[52]

As mentioned above, the 2008 reauthorization law (P.L. 110-378) required HHS, as of FY2010, to periodically submit to Congress an incidence and prevalence study of runaway and homeless youth ages 13 to 26, as well as the characteristics of a representative sample of these youth. As discussed, Congress appropriated funding to HUD for this purpose and findings were made available in 2017.[53]

The 2008 law also directed the Government Accountability Office (GAO) to evaluate the process by which organizations apply for BCP, TLP, and SOP, including HHS's response to these applicants. GAO submitted a report to Congress in May 2010 on its findings.[54] GAO found weaknesses in several of the procedures for reviewing grants, such as that peer reviewers for the grant did not always have expertise in runaway and homeless youth issues and feedback on grants was not provided in a permanent record. In addition, GAO found that HHS delayed telling successful grantees that the grant had been awarded to them. HHS has implemented the recommendations made in the report.

ADDITIONAL FEDERAL SUPPORT FOR RUNAWAY AND HOMELESS YOUTH

Since the creation of the Runaway and Homeless Youth Program, other federal initiatives have also established services for such youth.

---

52 HHS, *Promising Strategies to End Youth Homelessness, Report to Congress*, 2007, http://www.acf.hhs.gov/ programs/fysb/resource/end-youth-homelessness. This report was required under P.L. 108-96.

53 Matthew H. Morton, Amy Dworsky, and Gina M. Samuels, *Missed Opportunities: Youth Homelessness in America. National Estimates.*

54 U.S. Government Accountability Office, *Runaway and Homeless Youth Grants: Improvements Needed in the Grant Award Process*, GAO-10-335, May 2010, http://www.gao.gov/ products/GAO-10-335.

- Youth Homelessness Demonstration Program: The omnibus appropriations laws for FY2016 through FY2018 enabled HUD to set aside up to $33 million (FY2016), $43 million (FY2017), and $80 million (FY2018) from the Homeless Assistance Grants account to implement projects that demonstrate how a "comprehensive approach" can "dramatically reduce" homelessness for youth through age 24. The appropriations laws each fiscal year direct this funding to up to 10 communities with the FY2016 funding; up to 11 communities with the FY2017 funding, including at least five rural communities; and up to 25 communities with the FY2018 funding, including at least eight rural communities. HUD has allocated $33 million to 10 communities for FY2016 and plans to allocate $43 million for FY2017.[55]
- 100-Day Challenges to End Youth Homelessness: Since 2016, cities have partnered with public and private entities to accelerate efforts to prevent and end youth homelessness. A Way Home America and Rapid Results Institute, organizations that focus on pressing social problems, have provided support to the organizations. HHS provided training and technical assistance through RHYTTAC to the first three cities involved in the challenge: Los Angeles, CA; Cleveland, OH; and Austin, TX.[56] In general, participating communities have housed

---

[55] The sites funded with FY2016 appropriations include six urban areas (Anchorage, AK; San Francisco, CA; Watsonville/Santa Cruz City and County, CA; Connecticut; and Cincinnati/Hamilton County, OH) and four rural areas (Kentucky; Grand Traverse, Antrim, and Leelanau Counties, MI; and Ohio. See, HUD, "FY 2016 YHDP Debrief," January 13, 2017. The FY2017 funding announcement is available at HUD, "FY 2017 YHDP Application Resources," https://www.hudexchange.info/programs/yhdp/.

[56] HHS, ACF, ACYF, FYSB, "Follow the 100-Day Challenge to End Youth Homelessness," August 31, 2016, https://www.acf.hhs.gov/fysb/resource/100-day-challenge and CRS correspondence with HHS, Office of the Assistant Secretary for Legislation, December 2017.

homeless youth and have identified new housing options for this population.[57]

- Youth At-Risk of Homelessness: HHS has funded grants to build evidence on what works to prevent homelessness among youth and young adults who have child welfare involvement. HHS awarded funds to 18 grantees for a two-year planning period (2013-2015).[58] Six of the grantees received additional funding to refine and test their service models during a second phase (2015-2018). A subset of those grantees will then be selected to conduct a rigorous evaluation of their impact on homelessness.[59]

Educational Assistance

The McKinney-Vento Homeless Assistance Act of 1987 (P.L. 100-77), as amended, established the Education for Homeless Children and Youth program in ED.[60] This program assists state education agencies (SEAs) to ensure that all homeless children and youth have equal access to the same, appropriate education, including public preschool education, that is provided to other children and youth. Grants made by SEAs to local education agencies (LEAs) under this program must be used to facilitate the enrollment, attendance, and success in school of homeless children and youth. Program funds may be appropriated for

---

57 A Way Home America, "100-Day Challenge Overview," http://www.awayhomeamerica.org/100-day-challengeoverview/.

58 M.C. Bradley, Emily Knas, and Lisa Klein Vogel, *Youth At Risk of Homelessness: Lessons Learned from the Planning Phase*, Mathematica Policy Research for HHS, ACF, Office of Planning, Research, and Evaluation (OPRE), OPRE Report 2017-52a, August 2017.

59 HHS, ACF, OPRE, "Building Capacity to Evaluate Interventions for Youth/Young Adults with Child Welfare Involvement At-Risk of Homelessness (YARH), 2013-2019," https://www.acf.hhs.gov/opre/research/project/buildingcapacity-to-evaluate-interventions-for-youth-with-child-welfare-involvement-at-risk-of-homelessness.

60 For additional information about the program, see CRS Report RL30442, *Homelessness: Targeted Federal Programs*.

activities such as tutoring, supplemental instruction, and referral services for homeless children and youth, as well as providing them with medical, dental, mental, and other health services. Liaison staff for homeless children and youth in each LEA is responsible for coordinating activities for these youth with other entities and agencies, including local Basic Center and Transitional Living Program grantees. States that receive McKinney-Vento funds are prohibited from segregating homeless students from non-homeless students, except for short periods of time for health and safety emergencies or to provide temporary, special, supplemental services.[61]

Chafee Foster Care Independence Program[62]

Recently emancipated foster youth are vulnerable to becoming homeless. In FY2015, nearly 21,000 youth "aged out" of foster care.[63] The Chafee Foster Care Independence Program (CFCIP), created under the Chafee Foster Care Independence Act of 1999 (P.L. 106-169), provides states with funding to support youth who are expected to emancipate from foster care and former foster youth ages 18 to 21.[64] States are authorized to receive funds based on their share of the total number of children in foster care nationwide. However, the law's "hold harmless" clause precludes any state from receiving less than the amount of funds it received in FY1998 or $500,000, whichever is

---

61 The Individuals with Disabilities Education Act, last amended in 2004 (P.L. 108-446), includes provisions aimed at ensuring special education and related services for children with disabilities who are homeless or otherwise members of highly mobile populations. For additional information, see CRS Report R41833, *The Individuals with Disabilities Education Act (IDEA), Part B: Key Statutory and Regulatory Provisions*.

62 For additional information about the program, see CRS Report RL34499, *Youth Transitioning from Foster Care: Background and Federal Programs*.

63 HHS, ACF, ACYF, Children's Bureau, *AFCARS Report #22*.

64 For additional information on the Chafee Foster Care Independence Act, see CRS Report RL34499, *Youth Transitioning from Foster Care: Background and Federal Programs*.

greater.[65] The program specifies funding for transitional living services, and as much as 30% of the funds may be dedicated to room and board. The program is funded through mandatory spending, and as such $140 million is provided for the program each year through the annual appropriations process.

Discretionary Grants for Family Violence Prevention

The Family Violence Prevention and Services Act (FVPSA), Title III of the Child Abuse Amendments of 1984 (P.L. 98-457), authorized funds for Family Violence Prevention and Service grants that work to prevent family violence, improve service delivery to address family violence, and increase knowledge and understanding of family violence. From FY2007 to FY2009, one of these projects focused on runaway and homeless youth in dating violence situations through HHS's Domestic Violence/Runaway and Homeless Youth Collaboration on the Prevention of Adolescent Dating Violence initiative. The initiative was created because many runaway and homeless youth come from homes where domestic violence occurs and may be at risk of abusing their partners or becoming victims of abuse.[66] The initiative-funded projects carried out by faith-based and charitable organizations that advocated or provided direct services to runaway and homeless youth or victims of domestic violence. The grants funded training for staff at these organizations to enable them to assist youth in preventing dating violence. The initiative resulted in the development of an online toolkit for advocates in the runaway and homeless youth

---

[65] Prior to the enactment of P.L. 106-169, states were awarded a share of independent living funds—$70 million— based on the number of children receiving federal foster care payments in FY1984 under the Independent Living Program.

[66] HHS, ACF, ACYF, FYSB, *Discretionary Programs*, October 2010, https://www.acf.hhs.gov/fysb/fv-discretionary.

and domestic and sexual assault fields to help programs better address relationship violence with runaway and homeless youth.[67]

Appendix

Table A-1. Estimated Basic Center Funding by State and Territory, FY2016 and FY2017 (Dollars in thousands)

State/Territory	FY2016	FY2017
Alabama	$449,165	$587,980
Alaska	67,185	400,000
Arizona	796,151	799,558
Arkansas	575,781	551,261
California	4,474,818	5,758,877
Colorado	782,693	770,279
Connecticut	917,161	589,225
Delaware	400,000	109,103
District of Columbia	777,816	799,722
Florida	3,193,460	2,983,193
Georgia	1,390,114	1,227,663
State/Territory	FY2016	FY2017
Hawaii	195,000	200,000
Idaho	400,000	270,593
Illinois	2,227,522	2,107,492
Indiana	925,207	957,323
Iowa	424,650	312,882
Kansas	347,312	315,939
Kentucky	685,782	794,176
Louisiana	813,645	818,171
Maine	400,000	525,304
Maryland	400,000	396,715
Massachusetts	731,837	991,352
Michigan	2,293,327	2,227,988
Minnesota	1,134,550	835,852
Mississippi	600,000	407,623
Missouri	1,105,000	1,288,432
Montana	199,999	200,000

67 HHS, ACF, ACYF, FYSB, *Runaway & Homeless Youth and Relationship Violence Toolkit*, http://www.acf.hhs.gov/ programs/fysb/resource/rhy-dv-toolkit.

State/Territory	FY2016	FY2017
Nebraska	359,005	600,000
Nevada	452,845	402,398
New Hampshire	321,072	200,000
New Jersey	1,253,103	1,346,189
New Mexico	568,445	644,912
New York	2,492,126	2,705,737
North Carolina	1,199,080	1,236,815
North Dakota	399,025	200,000
Ohio	1,593,020	1,657,358
Oklahoma	556,761	833,844
Oregon	1,526,463	1,317,271
Pennsylvania	1,379,955	1,685,500
Rhode Island	129,906	0
South Carolina	400,000	399,828
South Dakota	527,000	321,429
Tennessee	1,109,203	600,000
Texas	3,226,678	2,751,415
Utah	800,000	442,891
Vermont	198,746	200,000
Virginia	870,026	999,999
Washington	766,901	969,997
West Virginia	258,385	128,769
Wisconsin	1,171,894	825,245
Wyoming	140,000	100,000
Total for States	*48,407,814*	*47,796,300*
American Samoa	199,768	70,000
Guam	100,000	127,000
Puerto Rico	287,000	400,000
Total for Territories	*586,768*	*597,000*
Total for States and Territories	$48,994,582	$48,393,300

Source: CRS correspondence with HHS, Office of the Assistant Secretary for Legislation, April 2018.

Note: The total does not include funding for technical assistance, research evaluation, demonstration projects, and program support. Rhode Island received $0 for FY2017 because the single application for funding from the state scored too low to be funded.

In: Children's Issues and Legislation ISBN: 978-1-53614-493-2
Editor: Christie Nguyen

Chapter 2

UNAUTHORIZED CHILDHOOD ARRIVALS: LEGISLATIVE ACTIVITY IN THE 115TH CONGRESS*

Andorra Bruno

SUMMARY

Legislative activity in the 115th Congress on unauthorized childhood arrivals (foreign nationals who as children were brought to live in the United States by their parents or other adults) comes in response to a decision announced by the Trump Administration on September 5, 2017, to terminate the Deferred Action for Childhood Arrivals (DACA) policy. The DACA policy was established by the Obama Administration in 2012 to provide eligible individuals with temporary protection against removal from the United States and work authorization. Initial DACA grants were for two years and could be renewed in two-year increments.

Under the Trump Administration's DACA phase-out plan announced in September 2017, a DACA beneficiary whose grant of deferred action

* This is an edited, reformatted and augmented version of Congressional Research Service, Publication No. R45139, dated March 22, 2018.

was due to expire on or before March 5, 2018, could submit a renewal request. A beneficiary whose DACA grant was due to expire after March 5, 2018, could not request a renewal and, thus, would lose DACA protection on the grant's expiration date. As of the date of this report, however, the Department of Homeland Security (DHS) continues to process requests to renew DACA, in accordance with federal court orders. According to DHS data, as of January 31, 2018, there were approximately 682,750 active DACA recipients.

Legislative proposals on unauthorized childhood arrivals in the 115th Congress build on related legislation introduced and considered in earlier Congresses. Past measures receiving action would have established a process for eligible unauthorized childhood arrivals to become U.S. lawful permanent residents (LPRs), who can live and work permanently in the United States. None of these measures were enacted. Bills introduced in the 115th Congress include measures to provide pathways to LPR status for certain unauthorized childhood arrivals, like the bills considered in past Congresses, as well as bills to provide more-limited DACA-like temporary protection from removal and employment authorization.

In February 2018, the Senate considered three proposals on unauthorized childhood arrivals as floor amendments to an unrelated bill (H.R. 2579). Each proposal would have established a pathway to LPR status for unauthorized childhood arrivals, although there were significant differences among them with respect to the eligible population, the legalization process and timeline, and the implications for the parents of beneficiaries. The Senate rejected motions to invoke cloture on any of the amendments. The House has not considered legislation on unauthorized childhood arrivals in the 115th Congress as of the date of this report.

INTRODUCTION

Unauthorized childhood arrivals is a general term used to describe foreign nationals who as children were brought to live in the United States by their parents or other adults. Sometimes referred to as *Dreamers*, they represent a subset of the larger unauthorized alien[1] population in the United States.[2] Many observers view them more

[1] *Alien* is a term used in immigration law to describe a person who is not a citizen or national of the United States. It is synonymous with *foreign national*.

[2] According to a preliminary estimate by the Pew Research Center, there were about 11.3 million unauthorized aliens living in the United States in 2016; Jens Manuel Krogstad, Jeffrey S.

sympathetically than other unauthorized aliens because they do not consider them responsible for their unlawful status, and they support establishing a process for them to obtain legal immigration status.[3] Others, however, argue that unauthorized childhood arrivals should not be afforded any special treatment under the immigration system.[4]

Bills on unauthorized childhood arrivals have been introduced in the House and the Senate since the 107th Congress. Legislative activity in the 115th Congress comes in response to a decision announced by the Trump Administration on September 5, 2017, to terminate the Deferred Action for Childhood Arrivals (DACA) policy established by the Obama Administration in 2012. Under the DACA policy, the Department of Homeland Security (DHS) granted deferred action to certain individuals without lawful immigration status who met a set of requirements, including initially entering the United States before age 16, continuously residing in the country since June 15, 2007, and being under age 31 as of June 15, 2012 (i.e., having a birthdate after June 15, 1981). DACA applicants also had to meet educational requirements (i.e., enrolled in school, completed high school, or obtained a general education development (GED) certificate) or military requirements (i.e., honorably discharged from the U.S. Armed Forces[5]), and were subject to specified criminal and security-related ineligibilities. Individuals granted deferred action under the DACA policy received protection

---

Passel, and D'Vera Cohn, *5 facts about illegal immigration in the U.S.*, Pew Research Center, April 27, 2017. The latest estimate from the Department of Homeland Security puts the 2014 resident unauthorized population at about 12.1 million; U.S. Department of Homeland Security, Office of Immigration Statistics, *Estimates of the Unauthorized Immigrant Population Residing in the United States: January 2014*, by Bryan C. Baker, July 2017. Analogous estimates of the "Dreamer" population are not available. There is no common definition of "Dreamer." Instead, Dreamer-related estimates tend to be tied to particular bills or proposals based on their specific eligibility criteria.

[3] See, for example, "Dreamers deserve to stay," [Charleston, SC] *Post and Courier*, January 2, 2018, https://www.postandcourier.com/opinion/editorials/dreamers-deserve-to-stay/article_2dc95b48-ea5a-11e7-a311- 53e107782eac.html.

[4] See, for example, Miriam Jordan, "Most Americans Want Legal Status for 'Dreamers.' These People Don't," *New York Times*, January 25, 2008, https://www.nytimes.com/2018/01/25/us/dreamers-opponents-daca-deal.html.

[5] *Armed Forces*, as defined in 10 U.S.C. §101(a)(4), means the Army, Navy, Air Force, Marine Corps, and Coast Guard.

against removal from the United States and could also receive work authorization. Initial DACA grants were for two years and could be renewed in two-year increments.[6]

Under the Trump Administration's DACA phase-out plan, as presented by DHS in September 2017, a DACA beneficiary whose grant of deferred action was due to expire on or before March 5, 2018, could submit a renewal request. A beneficiary whose DACA grant was due to expire after March 5, 2018, could not request a renewal and, thus, would lose DACA protection on the grant's expiration date. As of the date of this report, however, DHS continues to process requests to renew DACA, in accordance with federal court orders.[7] According to data published by DHS's U.S. Citizenship and Immigration Services (USCIS) in February 2018, the agency had approved a cumulative total of 807,447 initial DACA requests through January 31, 2018. As of that same date, there were approximately 682,750 active DACA recipients.[8]

In January 2018, the White House produced a "legislative framework" for immigration reform.[9] As part of that framework, the Trump Administration called on Congress to "provide legal status for DACA recipients and other DACA-eligible illegal immigrants."[10] Against this backdrop, the Senate considered several immigration

---

[6] See CRS Report R44764, *Deferred Action for Childhood Arrivals (DACA): Frequently Asked Questions*.

[7] See U.S. Department of Homeland Security, U.S. Citizenship and Immigration Services, *Deferred Action for Childhood Arrivals: Response to January 2018 Preliminary Injunction*, https://www.uscis.gov/humanitarian/deferredaction-childhood-arrivals-response-january-2018-preliminary-injunction.

[8] These data are available at Department of Homeland Security, U.S. Citizenship and Immigration Services, Immigration and Citizenship Data, https://www.uscis.gov/tools/reports-studies/immigration-forms-data, under the "DACA" tab.

[9] Statement from the Press Secretary on Immigration, January 24, 2018, https://www.whitehouse.gov/briefingsstatements/statement-press-secretary-21/.

[10] *White House Framework on Immigration Reform & Border Security*, fact sheet, January 25, 2018, https://www.whitehouse.gov/briefings-statements/white-house-framework-immigration-reform-border-security/.

proposals containing provisions on unauthorized childhood arrivals in February 2018. The House has not considered legislation on unauthorized childhood arrivals in the 115th Congress as of the date of this report.

LEGISLATIVE ACTIVITY PRIOR TO THE 115TH CONGRESS

Legislative proposals on unauthorized childhood arrivals in the 115th Congress build on related legislation introduced and considered in earlier Congresses. Measures receiving legislative action prior to the 115th Congress would have enabled eligible unauthorized childhood arrivals to become U.S. lawful permanent residents (LPRs).[11] Under most of these proposals, individuals meeting an initial set of criteria would have been granted some type of conditional or transitional legal status and then, after meeting additional criteria, would have been granted full-fledged LPR status. In the past, legislation proposing such a pathway to LPR status for unauthorized childhood arrivals was often referred to as the *DREAM Act*, whether or not a particular measure carried the bill title associated with that acronym (i.e., the Development, Relief, and Education for Alien Minors Act).[12]

Congressional action to grant LPR status to certain unauthorized childhood arrivals dates to the early 2000s. The Senate Judiciary Committee reported different DREAM Act bills in the 107th Congress

[11] *U.S. lawful permanent residents* (LPRs), also known as *immigrants* and *green card holders*, are foreign nationals who can live and work permanently in the United States. They can apply for U.S. citizenship under the naturalization provisions in the Immigration and Nationality Act (INA; Act of June 27, 1952, ch. 477, codified, as amended, at 8 U.S.C. §§1101 et seq.).

[12] In this report, the term DREAM Act is used to refer only to measures with the associated title.

(S. 1291) and the 108th Congress (S. 1545). Neither bill saw further action.[13]

Since then, legislative proposals on unauthorized childhood arrivals have been introduced as both stand-alone bills and parts of larger immigration reform bills.. While some of these measures have seen legislative action, none have been enacted. In the 109th Congress, the Senate passed a comprehensive immigration reform bill with a DREAM Act title (S. 2611); the House did not consider that bill. In the 110th Congress, there were unsuccessful efforts in the Senate to invoke cloture on a comprehensive immigration reform proposal that included a DREAM Act title (S. 1639) and to invoke cloture on a motion to proceed to a stand-alone DREAM Act bill (S. 2205).[14]

More recently, the House approved DREAM Act language as part of an unrelated bill in the 111th Congress (H.R. 5281); the Senate rejected a motion to invoke cloture on a motion to agree to the House-passed DREAM Act amendment. In the 113th Congress, the Senate passed a comprehensive immigration reform bill with DREAM Act provisions (S. 744); the House did not consider that bill.[15]

LEGISLATIVE ACTIVITY IN THE 115TH CONGRESS

A number of bills have been introduced in the 115th Congress to provide immigration relief to unauthorized childhood arrivals. Some of these measures would provide a pathway to LPR status, like the bills considered in past Congresses, while others would provide DACA-like temporary protection from removal and employment authorization. In

---

[13] See archived CRS Report RL31365, *Unauthorized Alien Students: Legislation in the 107th and 108th Congresses*.

[14] See archived CRS Report R43335, *Unauthorized Alien Students: Legislation in the 109th and 110th Congresses*. For general information about cloture, see CRS Report 98-425, *Invoking Cloture in the Senate*.

[15] See archived CRS Report RL33863, *Unauthorized Alien Students: Issues and "DREAM Act" Legislation*.

February 2018, the Senate considered three proposals on unauthorized childhood arrivals on the Senate floor. All three included a pathway to LPR status for successful applicants, although the particular provisions in the proposals differed. The discussion in this section is limited to provisions on unauthorized childhood arrivals in the relevant measures. It does not address any other provisions in these measures.

Measures Providing Temporary Protection from Removal

Legislation has been introduced in the 115th Congress that would provide temporary protection from removal and employment authorization to certain unauthorized childhood arrivals. For example, one proposal[16] would enable individuals who, on the date of enactment, have DACA protection and associated work authorization and meet additional requirements to obtain a new status that would afford them temporary protection from removal and work authorization. The new status would be granted for an initial period of three years and could be renewed in three-year increments.

Another proposal, which has been included in several bills,[17] would similarly provide eligible applicants with a new form of temporary protection from removal and employment authorization but would do so for a more-limited period of time (for three years after the date of enactment). It, however, would not apply only to current DACA recipients. Containing eligibility requirements broadly similar to those for DACA, this proposal would make temporary protection from removal and employment authorization available to DACA-eligible individuals who may never have applied for DACA protection.

---

[16] See H.R. 4760, Div. D, as introduced in the 115th Congress.

[17] See S. 127, S. 128/H.R. 496, S. 2192, Title IV, and S. 2464, Title II, as introduced in the 115th Congress.

Measures Providing Pathways to Lawful Permanent Residence

Multiple bills have been introduced in the 115th Congress to establish special pathways to LPR status for certain unauthorized childhood arrivals.[18] With some exceptions, these bills would first grant lawful permanent resident status on a conditional basis (conditional permanent resident status)[19] to unauthorized childhood arrivals who meet an initial set of requirements. In most cases, these requirements would include continuous presence in the United States since a specified date, initial U.S. entry before a specified age, specified educational (or in some cases, work or military) activity, and background checks, among others. All the bills would cover some individuals who do not satisfy the original DACA eligibility requirements concerning presence and age. The DACA policy, as noted, requires U.S. continuous residence since June 15, 2007, initial U.S. entry before age 16, and a birthdate after June 15, 1981. In contrast, some of the bills would require continuous presence since 2012, while others include later cutoff dates. Some of the bills would require initial entry before age 16, while others would require initial entry before age 18. Most would not set a maximum eligibility age.

Under the bills, aliens initially granted conditional permanent resident status would need to satisfy additional criteria in order to extend their conditional status (in the case of bills with two conditional periods) and to have the conditional basis of their status removed and

---

[18] These bills include H.R. 1468, H.R. 3440/S. 1615, H.R. 3591, H.R. 4796, S. 1852, S. 2199, and S. 2367, as introduced in the 115th Congress.

[19] Conditional permanent resident status is referenced in the INA. Under the INA, certain aliens obtaining lawful permanent resident status (such as certain alien spouses of U.S. citizens or LPRs and certain entrepreneurs) are considered to have obtained such status on a conditional basis. See INA §§216, 216a; 8 U.S.C. §§1186a, 1186b. Related DHS regulations can be found at 8 C.F.R. Part 216.

become full-fledged LPRs (in the case of all bills providing LPR pathways). The particular criteria in the bills differ, but in most cases, at either the conditional period extension stage or the condition removal stage, they include some number of years of education, military service, or work, among other requirements.

The bills also differ with respect to the length of their pathways to LPR status. For example, they would grant conditional permanent resident status for varying numbers of years. In addition, some bills would specify that an alien must be in conditional status for a minimum number of years before applying to remove the condition on his or her status and becoming a full-fledged LPR. Other bills include no such time requirements.

The bills include various provisions regarding residence requirements for naturalization, the process by which an LPR becomes a U.S. citizen. Under the Immigration and Nationality Act (INA), an alien typically has to reside in the United States in LPR status for five years before applying for U.S. citizenship.[20] Among the related provisions in some bills are sections stating that time in conditional permanent resident status would count toward the LPR residence requirement for naturalization.

February 2018 Senate Floor Action

In February 2018, the Senate considered four immigration proposals as floor amendments to an unrelated bill, the Broader Options for Americans Act (H.R. 2579). Three of the amendments included language on unauthorized childhood arrivals. The Senate rejected motions to invoke cloture on any of the amendments.[21]

---

[20] The INA is Act of June 27, 1952, ch. 477, codified, as amended, at 8 U.S.C. §§1101 et seq. The residence requirements for naturalization are in INA §316, 8 U.S.C. §1427.

[21] For general information about cloture, see CRS Report 98-425, *Invoking Cloture in the Senate*.

S.Amdt. 1955

S.Amdt. 1955 was entitled the Uniting and Securing America (USA) Act of 2018. Subtitle A contained provisions on unauthorized childhood arrivals.[22] It was substantively identical to Title I of a Senate bill (S. 2367) and a House bill (H.R. 4796) of the same name.

S.Amdt. 1955 would have established a mechanism for certain unauthorized childhood arrivals to become LPRs, in most cases through a two-stage process. In stage 1, an applicant would have been able to obtain lawful permanent resident status on a conditional basis (conditional permanent resident status) by meeting requirements including continuous presence in the United States since December 31, 2013; initial U.S. entry before age 18; no inadmissibility under specified grounds in the INA[23] and no other specified criminal ineligibilities; and either college admission, high school graduation or the equivalent, or secondary school enrollment or the equivalent. Among the other stage 1 requirements, the applicant would have had to clear security and law enforcement background checks, undergo a medical examination, and register under the Military Selective Service Act, if applicable. Conditional permanent resident status would have been valid for eight years, unless extended, and would have been subject to termination.

In stage 2, a conditional permanent resident would have had to meet a second set of requirements in order to have the conditional basis of his or her status removed and become a full-fledged LPR. These stage 2 requirements would have included either (1) acquisition of a college degree, or completion of at least two years in a postsecondary vocational program or a program for a bachelor's or higher degree; (2) service in the uniformed services[24] for the obligatory period; or (3)

---

[22] Other subtitles addressed border security, immigration judges, and other immigration issues.

[23] The INA enumerates grounds, including criminal grounds and security grounds, on which aliens are inadmissible to the United States and thus are ineligible to receive visas from the Department of State or to be admitted to the United States by DHS.

[24] *Uniformed services*, as defined in 10 U.S.C. §101(a)(5), means the Armed Forces (Army, Navy, Air Force, Marine Corps, and Coast Guard); the commissioned corps of the National

employment for at least three years and at least 80% of the time the alien had valid employment authorization. Other stage 2 requirements would have included satisfaction of the English language and civics requirements for naturalization[25] and completion of security and law enforcement background checks.

Under S.Amdt. 1955, a conditional permanent resident could have applied to have the condition on his or her status removed at any time after meeting the stage 2 requirements. The time spent in conditional status would have counted as time in LPR status for purposes of naturalization, but the alien could not have applied for naturalization while in conditional status. In addition, the bill would have provided that an alien meeting all the stage 1 and stage 2 requirements at the time of submitting his or her initial application would have been granted full-fledged LPR status directly (without first being granted conditional status).

On February 15, 2018, the Senate voted (52-47) not to invoke cloture on S.Amdt. 1955.

S.Amdt. 1958

S.Amdt. 1958 was entitled the Immigration Security and Opportunity Act.[26] Section 2 of the amendment would have established a two-stage pathway to LPR status for certain unauthorized childhood arrivals.[27] To obtain conditional permanent resident status in stage 1, an alien would have had to either be a DACA recipient or meet a set of requirements. These requirements would have included continuous presence in the United States since June 15, 2012; initial U.S. entry before age 18; no inadmissibility under specified grounds in the INA and no other specified criminal ineligibilities; and either satisfaction of

Oceanic and Atmospheric Administration; and the commissioned corps of the Public Health Service.

[25] See INA §312, 8 U.S.C. §1423.

[26] This amendment was considered on the Senate floor, as modified.

[27] Other sections of the amendment addressed border security and family-based immigration.

educational requirements like those under S.Amdt. 1955, or enlistment or service in the U.S. Armed Forces.[28]

Among the other requirements for conditional status, a non-DACA recipient would have had to meet a maximum age requirement—having a birthdate after June 15, 1974—and to have paid or arranged to pay any applicable federal tax liability, as specified. As under S.Amdt. 1955, all stage 1 applicants would have had to clear security and law enforcement background checks, undergo a medical examination, and register under the Military Selective Service Act, if applicable. Conditional permanent resident status under S.Amdt. 1958 would have been valid for seven years, unless extended, and would have been subject to termination.

In order to have the conditional basis of his or her status removed and become a full-fledged LPR, a conditional permanent resident would have had to meet a second set of requirements. These stage 2 requirements would have included (1) acquisition of a college degree or completion of at least two years in a program for a bachelor's or higher degree; (2) service in the uniformed services for at least two years, or, if the alien had been discharged, receipt of an honorable discharge; or (3) employment for at least three years and at least 75% of the time the alien had valid employment authorization. Other requirements would have included satisfaction of the English language and civics requirements for naturalization, completion of security and law enforcement background checks, payment or arrangement for payment of any applicable federal tax liability, and demonstration of good moral character during the entire conditional period.

Under S.Amdt. 1958, the time spent in conditional status would have counted as time in LPR status for purposes of naturalization. However, the amendment would have limited when beneficiaries could naturalize. In general, beneficiaries could not have been naturalized

---

[28] *Armed Forces*, as defined in 10 U.S.C. §101(a)(4), means the Army, Navy, Air Force, Marine Corps, and Coast Guard.

until 12 years after the date they received conditional permanent resident status. This period could have been reduced by up to two years for DACA recipients. S.Amdt. 1958 also would have limited the ability of the parents of its beneficiaries to obtain LPR status in the United States. The amendment would have specified that a parent could not obtain LPR status in the United States based on an immigrant petition filed by a child who received conditional permanent resident status if the parent had assisted in the child's unlawful entry into the United States.

On February 15, 2018, the Senate voted (54-45) not to invoke cloture on S.Amdt. 1958.

S.Amdt. 1959

Provisions on unauthorized childhood arrivals comprised Title III of S.Amdt. 1959, the SECURE and SUCCEED Act.[29] Title III, named the SUCCEED Act, was broadly similar to a Senate bill of the same name (S. 1852), although there were some key differences between the two measures.

S.Amdt. 1959 would have established a two-stage process for certain unauthorized childhood arrivals to obtain LPR status. Applicants who met an initial set of requirements would have been granted conditional *temporary* resident status.[30] These requirements would have included continuous presence in the United States since June 15, 2012; initial U.S. entry before age 16; a birthdate after June 15, 1981; no inadmissibility under specified grounds in the INA and no other specified criminal ineligibilities; and educational or military requirements based on the applicant's age on the date of enactment. Regarding the latter, aliens under age 18 would have had to be enrolled in or attending school. The requirements for applicants age 18 or older

---

[29] Other titles addressed border security, family-based immigration, and other immigration issues.

[30] Unlike conditional permanent resident status, conditional temporary resident status is not an existing immigration status. Legislation establishing a new immigration status typically sets forth the terms of that status in the text.

would have included either admission to college, high school graduation or the equivalent, or enlistment or service in the U.S. Armed Forces.

As under one or both of the other amendments discussed, all applicants would also have needed to clear security and law enforcement background checks; undergo a medical examination; register under the Military Selective Service Act, if applicable; and pay or arrange to pay any applicable federal tax liability, as specified. In addition, S.Amdt. 1959 included some requirements to obtain conditional status that were not found in the other amendments. Among them, an applicant age 18 or older would have had to acknowledge being notified that if he or she violated a term of conditional temporary resident status, he or she would be ineligible for any immigration relief or benefits, with limited exceptions.

Conditional temporary resident status would have been valid for an initial period of seven years or until the alien turned 18, if longer, and would have been subject to termination. Conditional temporary residents would have been eligible for employment authorization and enlistment in the U.S. Armed Forces, and could have traveled outside the United States and been permitted to return.

Under S.Amdt. 1959, an alien's initial period of conditional temporary residence would have been extended for five years if the alien met additional requirements, which would have included (1) college graduation or college attendance for at least eight semesters, (2) service in the U.S. Armed Forces for at least three years, or (3) a combination of college attendance, military service, and/or employment, as specified, for at least four years.

After seven years in conditional temporary resident status, an alien could have obtained LPR status if he or she satisfied another set of requirements. These included satisfaction of the English language and civics requirements for naturalization, completion of security and law enforcement background checks, payment of any applicable federal tax liability, and demonstration of good moral character during the entire conditional period.

Like S.Amdt. 1958, S.Amdt. 1959 would have limited both the ability of its beneficiaries to naturalize and the ability of the family members of its beneficiaries to obtain lawful immigration status under existing law. The provisions in S.Amdt. 1959, however, were more restrictive than those in S.Amdt. 1958. An individual would have had to wait at least seven years after being granted LPR status to apply for naturalization. S.Amdt. 1959 would also have provided that a parent or other family member of an alien granted conditional temporary resident status or LPR status could not gain any status under the immigration laws based on a parental or other family relationship.

On February 15, 2018, the Senate voted (39-60) not to invoke cloture on S.Amdt. 1959.

CONCLUSION

Each proposal on unauthorized childhood arrivals considered on the Senate floor in February 2018 would have established a pathway to LPR status for eligible beneficiaries. At the same time, there were significant differences among the proposals with respect to the eligible population, the legalization process and timeline, and the implications for the parents of beneficiaries. In addition, the proposals were parts of larger measures that addressed other components of the immigration system in different ways. It remains to be seen whether the 115th Congress will take up other immigration measures with provisions on unauthorized childhood arrivals along the same lines as the Senate amendments or opt to consider alternative approaches.

In: Children's Issues and Legislation ISBN: 978-1-53614-493-2
Editor: Christie Nguyen

Chapter 3

THE CHILD TAX CREDIT: LEGISLATIVE HISTORY*

Margot L. Crandall-Hollick

SUMMARY

The child tax credit was initially structured in the Taxpayer Relief Act of 1997 (P.L. 105-34) as a $500-per-child nonrefundable credit to provide tax relief to middle- and upper-middle-income families. Since 1997, various laws have modified key parameters of the credit, expanding the availability of the benefit to more low-income families while also increasing the value of the tax credit. The first significant change to the child tax credit occurred with the enactment of the Economic Growth and Tax Relief Reconciliation Act of 2001 (EGTRRA; P.L. 107-16). EGTRRA increased the amount of the credit over time to $1,000 per child and made it partially refundable under the earned income formula. The refundable portion of the credit—the amount that exceeds income tax liability—is often referred to as the additional child tax credit or ACTC.

* This is an edited, reformatted and augmented version of Congressional Research Service, Publication No. R45124, dated March 1, 2018.

Subsequent legislation enacted in 2003 and 2004 accelerated the implementation of the changes made under EGTRRA. In 2008 and 2009, Congress passed legislation—the Emergency Economic Stabilization Act of 2008 (EESA; P.L. 110-343) and the American Recovery and Reinvestment Act of 2009 (ARRA; P.L. 111-5)—that further expanded the availability and amount of the credit to taxpayers whose income was too low to either qualify for the credit or be eligible for the full credit. ARRA lowered the refundability threshold to its current level of $3,000 for 2009 through 2010. The ARRA provisions were subsequently extended several times and made permanent by the Protecting Americans from Tax Hikes (PATH) Act of 2015 (Division Q of P.L. 114-113).

At the end of 2017, Congress enacted P.L. 115-97 which, in addition to making numerous changes to the tax code, temporarily changed the child tax credit. Specifically, the law increased the credit for many (though not all) taxpayers by doubling the maximum amount of the credit (and increasing the maximum amount of the ACTC to $1,400), increasing the income at which the credit begins to phase out, and reducing the refundability threshold. In addition, this law temporarily modified the identification (ID) number requirement of the credit, requiring taxpayers to provide the Social Security number (SSN) for every child for whom they claimed the credit.

P.L. 115-97 also created a new temporary "family credit" for non-child credit eligible dependents (children ineligible for the child tax credit or older non-child dependents). Non-child credit eligible dependents excludes otherwise eligible dependents who are citizens of Mexico or Canada. The credit is equal to $500 per non-child credit eligible dependent. The amount is not annually adjusted for inflation. The phaseout parameters of the child credit (i.e., phaseout thresholds of $400,000 married filing jointly, $200,000 other taxpayers, 5% phaseout rate) apply to the family credit. The family credit is not annually adjusted for inflation.

All the modifications to the child tax credit and the new family credit are currently scheduled to expire at the end of 2025.

INTRODUCTION

The child tax credit was created in 1997 by the Taxpayer Relief Act of 1997 (P.L. 105-34) to help ease the financial burden that families incur when they have children. Over the past 20 years, legislative changes have significantly changed the credit, transforming it from a generally nonrefundable credit available only to the middle and upper-middle class, to a partially refundable credit that more low-income families are eligible to claim.

This report examines the legislative history of the credit, describing how the credit has changed over the past two decades as a result of different laws. The report includes a description of the recent legislative changes made to the credit by P.L. 115-97.

OVERVIEW

The child tax credit was initially structured in the Taxpayer Relief Act of 1997 (P.L. 105-34) as a $500-per-child nonrefundable credit to provide tax relief to middle- and upper-middle-income families. Since 1997, various laws have modified key parameters of the credit, expanding the availability of the benefit to more low-income families while also increasing the value of the tax credit. The first significant change to the child tax credit occurred with the enactment of the Economic Growth and Tax Relief Reconciliation Act of 2001 (EGTRRA; P.L. 107-16). EGTRRA increased the amount of the credit over time to $1,000 per child and made it partially refundable under the earned income formula. The refundable portion of the credit—the amount that exceeds income tax liability—is often referred to as the additional child tax credit or ACTC.

Subsequent legislation enacted in 2003 and 2004 accelerated the implementation of the changes made under EGTRRA. In 2008 and 2009, Congress passed legislation—the Emergency Economic Stabilization Act of 2008 (EESA; P.L. 110-343) and the American Recovery and Reinvestment Act of 2009 (ARRA; P.L. 111-5)—that further expanded the availability and amount of the credit to taxpayers whose income was too low to either qualify for the credit or be eligible for the full credit. ARRA lowered the refundability threshold to its current level of $3,000 for 2009 through 2010. The ARRA provisions were subsequently extended several times and made permanent by the Protecting Americans from Tax Hikes (PATH) Act of 2015 (Division Q of P.L. 114-113).

At the end of 2017, Congress enacted P.L. 115-97 which, in addition to making numerous changes to the tax code, temporarily changed the child tax credit. Specifically, the law increased the credit for many (though not all) taxpayers by doubling the maximum amount of the credit (and increasing the maximum amount of the ACTC to $1,400), increasing the income at which the credit begins to phase out, and reducing the refundability threshold as illustrated in *Table 1.* In addition, this law temporarily modified the identification (ID) number requirement of the credit, requiring taxpayers to provide the Social Security number (SSN) for every child for whom they claimed the credit.

Table 1. Overview of Key Aspects of the Child Tax Credit Under Current Law

Parameter	2018-2025	Post 2025[a]
Maximum credit per child	$2,000	$1,000
Maximum refundable portion of the credit per child (ACTC)[b]	$1,400	$1,000
Refundability Threshold	$2,500	$3,000
Refundability Rate	15%	15%
Phaseout Threshold	$200,000 unmarried taxpayer including married separate return $400,000 married joint return	$55,000 married separate return $75,000 unmarried taxpayer $110,000 married joint return
Phaseout Rate	5%	5%
Offset AMT Tax Liability	YES	YES

Source: Internal Revenue Code, 26 U.S.C. §24.

[a] Under current law, the temporary changes made to the child tax credit by P.L. 115-97 are scheduled to expire at the end of 2025.

[b] The refundable portion of the child tax credit is often referred to as the additional child tax credit or ACTC.

MAJOR LEGISLATIVE CHANGES MADE TO THE CHILD TAX CREDIT BETWEEN 1997 AND 2017

Below is a summary of major legislative changes made to the child tax credit between 1997 and 2017. These descriptions are preceded by an overview of policy debates that occurred immediately before enactment of the credit.

Before Enactment

The first child tax credit was enacted in 1997 as part of the Taxpayer Relief Act of 1997 (P.L. 105-34), but it was conceived years earlier and included in several different bills before it ultimately became law. In 1991, the bipartisan National Commission on Children,[1] which was established to provide solutions to a variety of problems facing children, recommended in its final report to the President the creation of a $1,000 refundable child tax credit for all children through age 18. The commission's proposed credit amount was indexed for inflation. The report cited slow wage growth, the increasing costs of living, and a rising tax burden for the average family as key factors leading to increased financial burdens on families with children.

The report's authors acknowledged that there were provisions in the tax code meant to address the increased financial burden to families that arose from having children, specifically the exemption for dependents. The dependent exemption was intended to provide economic relief to families with children by reducing taxable income by a fixed amount per dependent, and hence reducing tax liability. However, the amount of the exemption was fixed in nominal terms (i.e., not adjusted for

---

[1] For more information on the National Commission on Children, see its final report: National Commission on Children, *Beyond Rhetoric: A New American Agenda for Children and Families*, Washington, DC, 1991.

inflation) and the commission's report highlighted the fact that its real value had declined considerably since it was established in 1948.[2] The commission argued against simply increasing the amount of the dependent exemption, noting that such a policy would not provide adequate benefit to lower- and middle-income families. Specifically, the commission noted that the dependent exemption, similar to a tax deduction, provided greater monetary benefit to taxpayers with greater taxable income since it was proportional to a taxpayer's highest marginal tax bracket. And since the dependent exemption could not lower the tax liability of taxpayers who, due to low income, owed no federal income tax, it was unavailable to many families with children who the commission believed most needed economic assistance.

Three years later, in 1994, a child tax credit was included in legislation meant to enact key principles of the Contract with America, a list of policy proposals released by the Republican Party before the 1994 midterm elections. In the 104th Congress, both the American Dream Restoration Act (H.R. 6) and later the Tax Fairness and Deficit Reduction Act of 1995 (H.R. 1215), if they had been enacted, would have provided a $500-per-child nonrefundable[3] tax credit for children under 18 years. The credit would have begun to phase out for families with AGI above $200,000 (regardless of filing status). In response to the legislation that had been drafted in Congress, President Clinton proposed his own child tax credit during the 104th Congress in his Middle Class Bill of Rights Tax Relief Act of 1995. Under this

---

[2] In the Joint Committee on Taxation's (JCT's) explanation of the Taxpayer Relief Act of 1997, the committee cited the decline in the real value of the personal exemption by more than one-third over the prior 50 years as evidence of the tax system's failure to reflect a family's ability to pay. According to JCT, "The Congress believed that the individual income tax structure does not reduce tax liability by enough to reflect a family's reduced ability to pay taxes as family size increases. In part, this is because over the last 50 years the value of the dependent personal exemption has declined in real terms by over one third." For more information see U.S. Congress, Joint Committee on Taxation, JCS-23-97, *General Explanation of Tax Legislation Enacted in 1997*, December 17, 1997, pp. 6-7.

[3] The legislative language of the child tax credit included in H.R. 6 was drafted to create a new refundable credit. While the credit created by H.R. 6 could exceed a taxpayer's income tax liability, it could not exceed the sum of their income and Social Security taxes.

proposal, the child tax credit was a $300-per-child nonrefundable tax credit for tax years 1996 through 1998, increasing to $500 per child after 1998, with income phaseouts beginning at $60,000. The credit amounts were indexed for inflation. An eligible child was defined as being under 13 years of age.[4] President Clinton's proposal was estimated by the Department of the Treasury to cost $35.6 billion over five years, while the American Dream Restoration Act was estimated to cost $107 billion over the same time period.[5]

The Taxpayer Relief Act of 1997

After they did not reach an agreement in 1995, Congress and President Clinton revisited the topic of a child tax credit in 1997. The House, Senate, and Clinton Administration all proposed a $500 nonrefundable tax credit. A key distinction among the proposals centered on the interaction of the child tax credit with the EITC, which would have an impact on the availability of the child tax credit to lower-income taxpayers.[6] Both the Senate and House legislation proposed applying the nonrefundable child tax credit after the EITC had already reduced tax liability. President Clinton proposed the application of the child tax credit before the application of the EITC. For many low- and moderate-income taxpayers, claiming the EITC before the nonrefundable child tax credit reduced or eliminated their child tax credit. By contrast, claiming the nonrefundable child credit before the

---

[4] U.S. Congress, Joint Committee on Taxation, Background and Information Relating to Three Tax Cut Proposals for Middle Income Americans: A $500 per Child Tax Credit, A Reduction in the Marriage Penalty, and A Deduction for Education and Job Training Expenses, 104th Cong., 1st sess., March 15, 1995, p. 5.

[5] "Treasury Release Contrasting Revenue Costs of Clinton, GOP Tax Cuts," Tax Notes Today, LB1290, December 16, 1994.

[6] For more information on the differences in the House, Senate, and Clinton Administration proposals, see Table 1 in the archived CRS Report 97-687E, *Child Tax Credits: Comparison of Proposals for Low-Income Taxpayers*, by Gregg Esenwein and Jack Taylor, available by request.

EITC allowed the taxpayer to claim the full amount of the child tax credit they were eligible for and did not change the value of their EITC. For example, assume that in 1997 a two-parent, two-child family has $23,000 of income. This family would have an $825 tax liability before the application of credits. They would also be eligible for $1,325 in the EITC and, assuming the child credit was $500 per child, $1,000 of child tax credit. If the EITC was claimed before the child tax credit, this family's tax liability would be reduced to zero and they would receive the remainder of the EITC as a $500 refund. Since they had no tax liability, they could not claim the $1,000 of nonrefundable child tax credit. If, on the other hand, they claimed the child tax credit first, they could claim $825 of the nonrefundable child tax credit, reducing their tax liability to zero and then claim the full $1,325 of EITC as a refund.[7]

The child tax credit proposals differed in other ways, notably the interaction of the child tax credit with the child and dependent care credit, the age of a qualifying child, and the income phase-out levels and phase-out rates. Given that the child tax credit was part of a broader tax bill that had to meet budget rules, many of the specific details of the provision were likely agreed upon after evaluating their budgetary impact.

What emerged from the conference negotiations that year was the Taxpayer Relief Act of 1997 (P.L. 105-34), which established a child tax credit. The credit was structured as a $500 nonrefundable tax credit ($400 in 1998) for most families with qualifying children under 17. The credit phased out at a rate of $50 for every $1,000 by which a taxpayer's modified AGI exceeded thresholds based on filing status, namely $110,000 for taxpayers filing as married joint, $75,000 for taxpayers filing as head of household, and $55,000 for taxpayers filing

---

[7] All these figures are from Table 2 of the archived CRS Report 97-687E, *Child Tax Credits: Comparison of Proposals for Low-Income Taxpayers*, by Gregg Esenwein and Jack Taylor, available by request.

as married separate. The credit was refundable for taxpayers with three or more qualifying children and was calculated as the excess of a taxpayer's payroll taxes over their EITC (the alternative formula). Neither the credit amount nor the phaseout thresholds were indexed for inflation. The refundable portion of the credit was reduced by the amount of the taxpayer's alternative minimum tax (AMT).[8] In addition, the total amount by which personal nonrefundable credits (including the child tax credit) could reduce an individual's regular tax liability was limited.[9]

The Omnibus Consolidated and Emergency Supplemental Appropriations Act, 1999 (P.L. 105-277)

The Omnibus Consolidated and Emergency Supplemental Appropriations Act, 1999 (P.L. 105- 277), which was enacted shortly after the enactment of the Taxpayer Relief Act of 1997, repealed the provision that reduced the refundable portion of the child tax credit by the AMT for tax year 1998. In addition, this act allowed personal nonrefundable credits (including the child tax credit) to fully offset a taxpayer's regular income tax liability in 1998.[10]

---

[8] For more information on the AMT, see CRS Report RL30149, *The Alternative Minimum Tax for Individuals*, by Steven Maguire.

[9] The total amount of personal nonrefundable credits was limited to the extent that a taxpayer's regular tax liability exceeded their tentative minimum tax. The tentative minimum tax is an alternative tax calculated using a different definition of taxable income and different tax rates. For more information on the interaction of personal tax credits and the AMT, see CRS Report RL30149, *The Alternative Minimum Tax for Individuals*, by Steven Maguire.

[10] While personal nonrefundable credits could now offset both the regular tax and tentative minimum tax, they could only offset the tentative minimum tax by an amount less than or equal to their regular tax liability. Hence these credits could not offset the AMT (which is defined as the difference between the tentative minimum and regular tax liability). For more information on the interaction of personal tax credits and the AMT, see CRS Report RL30149, *The Alternative Minimum Tax for Individuals*, by Steven Maguire.

The Ticket to Work and Work Incentives Improvement Act of 1999 (P.L. 106-170)

The Ticket to Work and Work Incentives Improvement Act of 1999 (P.L. 106-170) extended the provision in P.L. 105-277 which allowed the nonrefundable personal credit to fully offset regular tax liability for one additional year, through the end of 1999. In addition, for tax years 2000 and 2001, the act included a provision which allowed taxpayers to use their personal nonrefundable credits (including the child tax credit) to not only offset their regular tax liability in full, but also their AMT. Finally, the act also extended for tax years 1999 through 2001 the prior-law repeal of the provision that reduced the refundable portion of the child tax credit by the AMT.

The Economic Growth and Tax Relief Reconciliation Act of 2001 (EGTRRA; P.L. 107-16)

The Economic Growth and Tax Relief Reconciliation Act of 2001 (EGTRRA; P.L. 107-16) made four significant changes to the child tax credit. First, EGTRRA increased the maximum amount of the credit per child in scheduled increments until it reached $1,000 per child in 2010. Second, EGTRRA made the credit refundable for families irrespective of size using the earned income formula. For tax years 2001 through 2004, the earned income formula set the amount of the refundable portion of the credit equal to 10% of a taxpayer's earned income in excess of $10,000, up to the maximum amount of the credit for that tax year. The refundability rate was scheduled to increase to 15% for tax years 2005 through 2010. The $10,000 threshold was indexed for inflation beginning in 2002. Third, EGTRRA allowed the child tax credit to offset AMT tax liability for tax years 2002 through 2010. Fourth, the law temporarily repealed the prior law provision that reduced the refundable portion of the child tax credit by the amount of the AMT. All the EGTRRA provisions were scheduled to expire at the end of 2010.

The Jobs and Growth Tax Relief Reconciliation Act of 2003 (JGTRRA; P.L. 108-27)

The Jobs and Growth Tax Relief Reconciliation Act of 2003 (JGTRRA; P.L. 108-27) temporarily accelerated the scheduled increase in the maximum credit amount. Specifically, while EGTRRA increased the maximum credit amount to $600 per child for 2003 and 2004, JGTRRA increased this amount to $1,000 per child for those two years. In the summer of 2003, the $400 increase in the credit for 2003 was paid in advance from the Department of the Treasury to many families who qualified for the child tax credit. These direct payments were distributed based on information contained on taxpayers' 2002 income tax returns. The JGTRRA provisions were scheduled to expire after 2004, and the child tax credit would have reverted to its scheduled level under EGTRRA—$700 per child in 2005.

The Working Families Tax Relief Act of 2004 (WFTRA; P.L. 108-311)

In September 2004, Congress passed the Working Families Tax Relief Act of 2004 (WFTRA; P.L. 108-311), which further accelerated the implementation of key provisions of EGTRRA. This act extended the maximum amount of the credit established under JGTRRA, $1,000 per child, through 2009. For 2010, the EGTRRA provisions would apply and the maximum amount of the credit would remain $1,000 per child. In addition, WFTRA increased the refundability rate to 15% for

2004. Under EGTRRA, the refundability rate would remain at 15% from 2005 through 2010.

WFTRA also contained a provision that allowed combat pay to be included as part of earned income for purposes of computing refundability of the child tax credit. As more soldiers began to see combat due to the wars in Iraq and Afghanistan, they started receiving combat pay. Income earned by members of the armed services in a combat zone is generally excluded from taxation. This exclusion benefits taxpayers who have positive tax liability and reduces the taxes they owe. However, for some lower-income members of the Armed Forces, the exclusion resulted in earnings being too low to qualify for the refundable portion of the child tax credit. The inclusion of combat pay as earned income for purposes of calculating the refundable child tax credit under WFTRA meant that the earnings of some military families would increase above the refundability threshold, ultimately resulting in larger child tax credit refunds. This change was for 2004 through 2010, and was scheduled to expire, along with other provisions of EGTRRA, at the end of 2010.

The Emergency Economic Stabilization Act of 2009 (EESA; Division A of P.L. 110-343)

In October 2008, Congress passed the Emergency Economic Stabilization Act of 2009 (EESA; P.L. 110-343) in response to the financial and housing crisis. The law included a provision to lower the refundability threshold for the child tax credit for 2008 from $12,050[11] to $8,500. In the absence of any additional congressional action, the refundability threshold was scheduled to increase to $12,550 in 2009.

[11] The $10,000 threshold established by EGTRRA, adjusted for inflation.

The American Recovery and Reinvestment Act of 2009 (ARRA; P.L. 111-5)

In early 2009, Congress began to debate different legislative proposals for economic stimulus. Part of that debate concerned changing the refundability threshold of the child tax credit. The House proposed[12] reducing the refundability threshold to zero for 2009 and 2010, while the Senate proposed[13] lowering the refundability threshold to $8,100 over the same time period. The House's proposed changes to the child tax credit were estimated to cost $18.3 billion over 10 years, in comparison to $7.2 billion for the Senate proposal. The provision took its final shape during the meetings between the Senate and the House conferees.[14] In February 2009 Congress passed the American Recovery and Reinvestment Act of 2009 (ARRA; P.L. 111-5), which ultimately reduced the refundability threshold to $3,000 for 2009 and 2010. This proposal was estimated to cost $14.8 billion over 10 years.[15]

The Tax Relief, Unemployment Insurance Reauthorization, and Job Creation Act of 2010 (P.L. 111-312)

At the end of 2010, both the EGTRRA and ARRA provisions of the child tax credit (see *Table 2*) were scheduled to expire. Since ARRA's changes to the refundability threshold built upon changes made by EGTRRA, the expiration of EGTRRA would effectively terminate the expansion of refundability made by the 2009 stimulus law (ARRA). Absent an extension of EGTRRA, the maximum amount of the child

---

[12] H.R. 1 that passed the House on January 28, 2009.

[13] S.Amdt. 570 in the nature of a substitute to H.R. 1, which passed the Senate on February 10, 2009.

[14] See the Conference Report H.Rept. 111-16.

[15] U.S. Congress, Joint Committee on Taxation, JCX-19-09, *Estimated Budget Effects Of The Revenue Provisions Contained In The Conference Agreement For H.R. 1, The "American Recovery And Reinvestment Tax Act Of 2009,"* February 12, 2009, p. 1.

tax credit would have reverted to $500 per child, the credit would only have been refundable to families with three or more children using the alternative formula, and the amount of the child tax credit would not have been allowed in full against the AMT. In December 2010, Congress passed the Tax Relief, Unemployment Insurance Reauthorization, and Job Creation Act of 2010 (P.L. 111-312), which extended both the EGTRRA provisions of the child tax credit[16] and the expansion of refundability from ARRA for two years through the end of 2012.

The American Taxpayer Relief Act of 2012 (P.L. 112-240; ATRA)

At the end of 2012, Congress passed the American Taxpayer Relief Act of 2012 (P.L. 112-240; ATRA). This law made the EGTRRA changes to the child tax credit permanent and extended the $3,000 refundability threshold enacted as part of ARRA for five years, through the end of 2017.

The Protecting Americans from Tax Hikes (PATH) Act of 2015 (Division Q of P.L. 114-113)

The Protecting Americans from Tax Hikes (PATH) Act of 2015 (Division Q of P.L. 114-113) made the ARRA modification to the child tax credit—the $3,000 refundability threshold— permanent.

[16] This includes the inclusion of combat pay as part of earned income for purposes of calculating refundability under the earned income formula created by EGTRRA. In addition this law extended for two years (through the end of 2012) the EGTRRA repeal of a prior-law provision that reduced the refundable portion of the child credit by the amount of the AMT and it extended the EGTRRA provision which allowed the child tax credit to offset a taxpayer's AMT.

In addition, the PATH Act modified the taxpayer identification requirement for the credit to specify an ID requirement for each child for whom the credit is claimed. Specifically, a taxpayer claiming the credit must provide a valid Taxpayer Identification Number (TIN) for each qualifying child on their federal income tax return. Valid TINs include individual taxpayer identification numbers (ITINs),[17] Social Security numbers (SSNs), and adoption taxpayer identification numbers (ATINs).[18] ITINs are issued by the Internal Revenue Service (IRS) to noncitizens who do not have and are not eligible to receive SSNs. ITINs are supplied solely so that noncitizens are able to comply with federal tax law, and do not affect immigration status. The law also required that the TIN—for both the qualifying child and the taxpayer—be issued on or before the due date of the return.

The 2017 Tax Revision (P.L. 115-97)

At the end of 2017, Congress passed the 2017 tax revision[19] (P.L. 115-97) which made numerous changes to the federal income tax for individuals and businesses,[20] including temporarily expanding the child tax credit. These temporary changes to the child tax credit are summarized in *Table 1*.

---

[17] For more information on the child tax credit and ITIN filers, see CRS Report R44420, *Individual Taxpayer Identification Number (ITIN) Filers and the Child Tax Credit: Overview and Legislation*, by Margot L. CrandallHollick and Erika K. Lunder.

[18] For more information on ATINs, see the IRS Question and Answer on ATINs, at https://www.irs.gov/individuals/adoption-taxpayer-identification-number.

[19] The bill was originally short titled "The Tax Cuts and Jobs Act." The short title of the bill was stricken before final passage because it violated what is known as the Byrd rule, a procedural rule that can be raised in the Senate when bills, like the tax bill, are considered under the process of reconciliation. The final official title of the law is "To provide for reconciliation pursuant to titles II and V of the concurrent resolution on the budget for fiscal year 2018." For more information on the Byrd rule, see CRS Report RL30862, *The Budget Reconciliation Process: The Senate's "Byrd Rule,"* by Bill Heniff Jr.

[20] For more information on the changes made to the tax code by P.L. 115-97 see CRS Report R45092, *The 2017 Tax Revision (P.L. 115-97): Comparison to 2017 Tax Law*, coordinated by Molly F. Sherlock and Donald J. Marples.

The law doubled the maximum amount of the credit from $1,000 to $2,000 per qualifying child and increased the maximum amount of the refundable portion of the credit (the additional child tax credit or ACTC) from $1,000 per qualifying child to $1,400 per qualifying child. While in effect, the expanded ACTC amount can be annually adjusted for inflation using the chained consumer price index. (The law uses an indexing convention that rounds the $1,400 amount to the next lowest multiple of $100.) The law also lowered the income level at which taxpayers could begin receiving the ACTC from $3,000 to $2,500. Finally, the law increased the income level at which the credit begins to phase out from $75,000 to $200,000 for unmarried taxpayers, and from $110,000 to $400,000 for married taxpayers filing joint returns. Aside from the inflation adjustment of the ACTC, all other parameters of the child tax credit are not adjusted for inflation.

In addition, the law temporarily required taxpayers to provide an SSN associated with work authorizations for any child for whom they claim the credit. The SSN must be issued before the due date of the tax return. Failure to provide the child's current SSN could result in the taxpayer being denied the credit (both the nonrefundable and refundable portions of the credit). The law did not change the ID requirement for the taxpayer.

Finally, the law created a new temporary "family credit" for non-child credit eligible dependents (children ineligible for the child tax credit or older non-child dependents). Non-child credit eligible dependents excludes otherwise eligible dependents who are citizens of Mexico or Canada. The credit is equal to $500 per non-child credit eligible dependent. The amount is not annually adjusted for inflation. The phaseout parameters of the child credit (e.g., phaseout thresholds of $400,000 married filing jointly, $200,000 other taxpayers, 5% phaseout rate) apply to the family credit. The family credit is not annually adjusted for inflation.

All the modifications to the child tax credit and the new family credit are currently scheduled to expire at the end of 2025.

Table 2. Changes to the Child Tax Credit Made by Legislation 1997-2017

	1997	*1999*	*2001*	*2003*	*2004*	*2008*	*2009*	*2010*	*2013*	*2015*	*2017*
Parameter	*P.L. 105-34*	*P.L. 106-170*	*P.L. 107-16(EGTRRA)*	*P.L. 108-27(JGTRRA)*	*P.L. 108-311(WFTRA)*	*P.L. 110-343(EESA)*	*P.L. 111-5(ARRA)*	*P.L. 111-312*	*P.L. 112-240(ATRA)*	*P.L. 114-113*	*P.L. 115-97*
Maximum Credit per Child	$400 (1998) $500 (after)	*	$600 (2001-04)$700 (2005-08)$800 (2009)$1,000 (2010)	$1,000 (2003-04)	$1,000 (2005-10)	*	*	$1,000 (2011-12)	$1,000 (permanent)	*	$2,000
Inflation adj.	NO	*	*	*	*	*	*	*	*	*	NO
Refundable[a]	NO	*	YES (2001-2010)	*	*	*	*	YES (2011-2012)	YES (permanent)	*	*
Max Refundable Credit per Child	na	na	same as max credit per child	*	*	*	*	*	*	*	$1,400[e] (2018-2025)
Refund-ability Threshold	na	*	$10,000 (2001-10)	*	*	$8,500 (2008)	$3,000 (2009-10)	$3,000 (2011-12)	$3,000 (2013-2017) $10,000	$3,000 permanent	$2,500 (2018-2025)
Inflation adj.	na	*	YES (2002-10)	*	*	NO	NO (2009-2010)	NO (2011-12)	NO (2013-2017)YES thereafter	NO	NO

Table 2. (Continued)

	1997	*1999*	*2001*	*2003*	*2004*	*2008*	*2009*	*2010*	*2013*	*2015*	*2017*
Parameter	*P.L. 105-34*	*P.L. 106-170*	*P.L. 107-16(EGTRRA)*	*P.L. 108-27(JGTRRA)*	*P.L. 108-311(WFTRA)*	*P.L. 110-343(EESA)*	*P.L. 111-5(ARRA)*	*P.L. 111-312*	*P.L. 112-240(ATRA)*	*P.L. 114-113*	*P.L. 115-97*
Refund-ability Rate	na	*	10% (2001-04)15% (2005-10)	*	15% (2004-2010)	*	*	15% (2011-12)	15% (permanent)	*	*
Phaseout Threshold[b]	$55,000 MFS $75,000 HOH$110,00 MFJ	*	*	*	*	*	*	*	*	*	$200,000MFS $200,000HOH $400,000MFJ
Phaseout Rate	5%	*	*	*	*	*	*	*	*	*	*
Offset AMT	NO	YES(2000-01)	YES (2002-10)	*	*	*	*	YES(2011-2012)	YES (permanent)	*	*
Revenue Effect	-$183.38 billion (1997-07)	-$2.89 billion[c] (2000-09)	-$171.78 billion (2001-11)	-$32.49 billion (2003-13)	-$63.77 billion (2005-14)	-$3.13 billion (2009-18)	-$14.83 billion (2009-19)	-$91.44 billion (2011-20)	-$405.01 billion (2013-2022)	-$87.84billion (2016-2025)	-573.40billion (2018-2027)[d]

Source: Joint Committee on Taxation.

Notes: *-Indicates unchanged from prior law. Except as otherwise noted, revenue effects reflect the cost of the child tax credit provisions exclusively.

[a] Prior to EGTRRA, the child credit was only refundable for families with three or more children under the alternative formula.

[b] MFS, HOH, and MFJ refer to tax filing status, specifically: MFS: married filing separately; HOH: head of household; MFJ: married filing joint.

[c] This law allowed nonrefundable personal credits (including the child tax credit) to offset the regular tax in full (without regard to the tentative minimum tax) for tax year 1999 (which was an extension of a provision in P.L. 105-277). For tax years 2000 and 2001, this law included a special provision that allowed

personal nonrefundable credits in full against regular tax and the AMT. The revenue effect reflects the effect of these provisions on personal nonrefundable credit, and is not limited to their effect on the child tax credit.

[d] This estimate includes the budgetary impact of the non-refundable $500 credit for non-child credit dependents. It does not include the estimated $29.8 billion in savings over the 2018 to 2027 budgetary window from the Social Security number (SSN) ID requirement for qualifying children.

[e] Beginning in 2019, $1,400 is adjusted for inflation using the chained consumer price index. Adjustments are rounded down to the next lowest multiple of $100. The other parameters of the credit are not adjusted for inflation by P.L. 115-97.

In: Children's Issues and Legislation ISBN: 978-1-53614-493-2
Editor: Christie Nguyen

Chapter 4

THE MISSING AND EXPLOITED CHILDREN'S (MEC) PROGRAM: BACKGROUND AND POLICIES*

Adrienne L. Fernandes-Alcantara

SUMMARY

Beginning in the late 1970s, highly publicized cases of children who were abducted, sexually abused, and sometimes murdered prompted policymakers and child advocates to declare a missing children problem. At that time, about 1.8 million children annually were reported to the police as missing. More recent data indicate that the number and rate at which children go missing has declined. A survey from 2013 provides the most recent and comprehensive information on missing children. The data show that about 238,000 children (3.1 per 1,000 children) were reported to law enforcement by their caretakers that year as missing due to a family or nonfamily abduction; running away or being forced to

* This is an edited, reformatted and augmented version of Congressional Research Service, Publication No. RL34050, dated February 8, 2018.

leave home; becoming lost or injured; or for benign reasons, such as a miscommunication about schedules.

As a policy issue, missing children are often included in discussions of sexual victimization. Children who go missing—as well as children who are not missing—may be sexually exploited. A study that examined the prevalence of children's exposure to violence in 2008 found that 1 in 16 (6.1%) surveyed children were sexually victimized in the past year and nearly 1 in 10 (9.8%) were sexually victimized at some point over their lifetimes.

Recognizing the need for greater federal coordination of local and state efforts to recover missing and exploited children, Congress passed the Missing Children's Assistance Act (P.L. 98-473) in 1984. The act directed the U.S. Department of Justice's (DOJ's) Office of Juvenile Justice and Delinquency Prevention (OJJDP) to establish a national resource center for missing and exploited children, among other related activities. The Missing Children's Assistance Act has been amended multiple times, most recently in 2013 (P.L. 113-38).

Activities authorized under the Missing Children's Assistance Act and selected other laws are collectively referred to as the Missing and Exploited Children's (MEC) program. The program includes the following components:

- The National Center for Missing and Exploited Children (NCMEC): Since 1984, NCMEC has served as the national resource center and has carried out many of the objectives of the Missing Children's Assistance Act in collaboration with OJJDP.
- The Internet Crimes Against Children (ICAC) Task Force program: This program assists state and local enforcement cyber units in investigating online child sexual exploitation. It was authorized under the PROTECT Our Children Act of 2008 (P.L. 110-401), as amended.
- Training and technical assistance for state AMBER (America's Missing: Broadcast Emergency Response) Alert systems: AMBER Alerts publicly broadcast bulletins in the most serious child abduction cases. The AMBER Alert program is authorized under the PROTECT Act (P.L. 108-21).
- Other initiatives: These include training and technical assistance on investigating and preventing child victimization. They also include support to membership-based nonprofit missing and exploited children's organizations. These initiatives are authorized by the Missing Children's Assistance Act.

FY2017 appropriations to DOJ for the MEC program were $72.5 million, of which $28.3 million was for NCMEC, $27.6 million was for the ICAC Task Force program, $2.4 million was for the AMBER Alert program, and $4.2 million was for other initiatives. The remaining amount was allocated for other DOJ activities.

INTRODUCTION

The Missing and Exploited Children's (MEC) program—administered by the Department of Justice's (DOJ's) Office of Juvenile Justice and Delinquency Prevention (OJJDP) in the Office of Justice Programs (OJP)—seeks to prevent cases of missing and sexually exploited children and to support communities in responding to such cases. The program is composed of activities that are authorized under multiple laws, and includes the following components:

- The National Center for Missing and Exploited Children (NCMEC) is a nonprofit organization in Alexandria, VA, that serves as a resource center for law enforcement agencies working on cases of missing and exploited children, the families of child victims, and the public more broadly. NCMEC personnel take reports of missing and exploited children through a hotline and online portal. NCMEC also provides technical assistance to locate abductors and recover missing children, and help with identifying child victims of sexual exploitation. In recent years, funding for NCMEC has been approximately $28 million annually.
- The Internet Crimes Against Children (ICAC) Task Force program funds state and local law enforcement units in investigating online child sexual exploitation. The program also includes the National ICAC Data System (NIDS), which is used by law enforcement agencies to coordinate information about perpetrators who sexually abuse children on the Internet and to recover these children. Recent funding for the ICAC program has been approximately $27 million annually.

- Under the AMBER Alert (America's Missing: Broadcast Emergency Response) program, DOJ supports a grantee that provides technical assistance to states in alerting the public when children are abducted and believed to be in imminent danger. AMBER Alert technical assistance has been funded at approximately $2 million annually in recent years.
- The MEC program also provides grants for training and technical assistance on child victimization and related supports. Training and technical assistance is delivered via a grantee that provides assistance through classroom instruction, web-based learning, and in-person support. These grants can vary from year to year, and recent funding has been approximately $4 million annually.

This report covers selected aspects of research and policy concerning missing and exploited children. It begins with background on federal involvement in missing children's issues. The next section includes definitions and approximate numbers of children who are missing and sexually exploited. The report then provides information about each component of the MEC program.[1]

BACKGROUND

Congress has long been concerned about missing children. In the early 1970s, Congress held hearings about a subset of these children—those who had run away from home. Testimony focused on the

---

[1] Grants for NCMEC, training and technical assistance, and related supports are authorized under the Missing Children's Assistance Act (P.L. 98-413), as amended (34 U.S.C. 11293 et seq.; Chapter 111, Juvenile Justice and Delinquency Prevention). The ICAC Task Force program is authorized under the PROTECT Our Children Act of 2008 (P.L. 110-401), as amended (34 U.S.C. §§21112-21117; Chapter 211, Combating Child Exploitation). The AMBER Alert program is authorized under the PROTECT Act (P.L. 108-21) (34 U.S.C. §20501; Chapter 205, AMBER Alert).

interaction that runaway youth had with police and their increasing reliance on social service agencies for support. These hearings and related activity led to the passage of the Runaway Youth Act of 1974 as Title III of the Juvenile Justice and Delinquency Prevention Act (P.L. 93-415). The act, as amended, authorizes assistance to runaway and homeless youth through shelters and other services.[2]

Beginning in the late 1970s, highly publicized cases of children who were abducted, sexually abused, and sometimes murdered prompted policymakers and child advocates to declare a missing children problem. At that time, many of the victims' families and communities perceived that kidnappings were becoming more commonplace. Prominent cases of missing children were highly publicized and a docudrama, "Adam," depicted the story of abducted six-year-old Adam Walsh, son of John and Revé Walsh.[3] Testimony at congressional hearings about missing children further reinforced the perception of a missing children problem. Witnesses testified that as many as 1.8 million children were missing. They also highlighted the accompanying sexual exploitation that children often experienced during missing episodes.[4] In some parts of the country, nonprofit organizations formed by the parents of missing children were often the only entities that organized recovery efforts and provided counseling for victimized families.

Congress responded by passing two bills, both of which were enacted. The Missing Children Act of 1982 (P.L. 97-292) directed the Attorney General to keep records on missing children in the National Crime Information Center's (NCIC's) Missing Persons File, maintained by the Federal Bureau of Investigation (FBI), and to disseminate those

---

[2] For further information, see CRS Report RL33785, *Runaway and Homeless Youth: Demographics and Programs*, by Adrienne L. Fernandes-Alcantara.

[3] Martin L. Forst and Martha-Elin Blomquist, *Missing Children* (New York: Lexington Books, 1991), pp. 56-66.

[4] U.S. Congress, Senate Committee on the Judiciary, Subcommittee on Juvenile Justice, *Missing Children's Assistance Act* hearing, 98th Congress, 2nd sess., February 7, 1984 (Washington, DC: GPO, 1984).

records to state and local agencies.[5] That law neither created new federal jurisdiction over missing children's programs nor required federal law enforcement officials to coordinate missing children efforts. Two years later, the Missing Children's Assistance Act (P.L. 98-473) was enacted. It directed OJJDP to lead federal efforts to recover missing children and establish a national resource center on missing children. NCMEC has served as the resource center since 1984. The Missing Children's Assistance Act has been amended multiple times to further specify the responsibilities of OJJDP and NCMEC in responding to missing and exploited children. For example, OJJDP supports training and technical assistance to strengthen community responses to child victimization cases, among other activities. Current funding authorization under the Missing Children's Assistance Act is \$40 million for each of FY2014 through FY2018. Of this amount, up to \$32.2 million is to be allotted to NCMEC.[6] (The *Appendix* provides a description of the original act and its amendments.)

The federal government has since provided additional resources in support of missing and exploited children. Selected activities have been subsumed under the MEC program. DOJ first funded the ICAC Task Force program in 2008 to support state and local law enforcement agencies in combatting online enticement of children and the proliferation of pornography. The PROTECT Our Children Act of 2008 (P.L. 110-401) formally authorized the program. This law provided two authorizations for the ICAC Task Force program—one for \$60 million for FY2009- FY2013 for ICAC activities generally, including grants for ICAC task forces, and one for \$2 million for each of FY2009-FY2016 for the National ICAC Data System, which facilitates online law

---

[5] The NCIC is a digital index of information on crimes and criminals accessed by federal, state, and local law enforcement officials. The FBI authorizes the National Central Bureau of Interpol to input missing-child cases into the Missing Person File where no U.S. law enforcement agency jurisdiction exists (34 U.S.C. §41308).

[6] NCMEC coordinates and is involved with several federal activities relating to missing and exploited children. Some of these activities are funded from sources other than the MEC program, though it provides the largest share of federal funds for NCMEC.

enforcement investigations of child exploitation. The Child Protection Act of 2012 (P.L. 112- 206), signed into law on December 7, 2012, authorized annual appropriations of $60 million for the ICAC Task Force program generally (including the data system and the National Strategy for Child Exploitation Prevention and Interdiction, discussed later in this report) through FY2018. The Providing Resources, Officers, and Technology to Eradicate Cyber Threats to Our Children Act of 2017 (PROTECT Our Children Act of 2017, P.L. 115-82) extended annual authorizations of $60 million for the ICAC Task Force program generally through FY2022.

Separately, OJP first provided funding ($10 million in discretionary appropriations) in 2002 for states and localities to develop AMBER Alert programs. The Prosecutorial Remedies and Other Tools to End the Exploitation of Children Today Act of 2003 (PROTECT Act, P.L. 108-21), enacted in 2003, directed the Attorney General to create a national AMBER Alert program, including appointing a coordinator and developing standards for issuing an alert.[7] P.L. 108-21 also authorized funding in FY2004 for activities to support states in developing AMBER Alert communication plans and technologies. As discussed in more detail later in this report, the MEC program has used continuous appropriations since FY2004 to provide technical assistance to states' AMBER Alert plans and in responding to child abductions.

DEMOGRAPHICS OF MISSING AND EXPLOITED CHILDREN

Overview

Children who go missing—as well as children who are not missing—may be sexually exploited. Missing children and sexually exploited children are distinct but overlapping populations. The term

[7] 34 U.S.C. §20501.

"missing child" is defined under the Missing Children's Assistance Act as an individual under age 18 whose whereabouts are unknown to that individual's legal custodian.[8] Although the Missing Children's Assistance Act does not define child sexual exploitation, both criminal and civil federal statutes specify acts of sexual exploitation for purposes of prosecuting offenders and providing minimum standards of child abuse for states to use in their own definitions of child abuse.[9]

The actual number of children who are currently missing or sexually exploited is unknown; however, studies have estimated the rate of children who are missing or sexually exploited (as discussed in more detail below).

Missing Children

The Missing Children's Assistance Act requires OJJDP to conduct incidence studies of the number of missing children, the number of children missing due to a stranger abduction or parental abduction, and the number of missing children who are recovered.[10] Since the act's

---

[8] This definition is codified at 34 U.S.C. §11292. It was changed in 2006 under P.L. 109-248. Previously, the definition included an individual under age 18 whose whereabouts are unknown to that individual's legal custodian if (1) the circumstances surrounding his or her disappearance indicate that the individual may possibly have been removed by another individual from the control of his or her legal custodian without the custodian's consent, or (2) the circumstances of the case strongly indicate that the individual is likely to be abused and sexually exploited.

[9] For example, Title 18 of the U.S. Code includes multiple crimes involving the sexual exploitation of children, such as commerce in child pornography; transferring obscene material to a child by mail or through interstate or foreign travel; traveling abroad to engage in a sexual act with a child; and using a misleading domain name, words, or digital images on the Internet with the intent to deceive a minor into viewing material that is harmful to that minor. Most federal criminal statutes on child sexual exploitation are in Chapters 71, 77, 109A, 109B, 110, and 117. In addition, Title 42 of the U.S. Code, at 42 U.S.C. §5106g, provides definitions related to child sexual exploitation for purposes of abuse and neglect. Title 34 of the U.S. Code requires individuals convicted of specified crimes against children or sexually violent crimes to register their addresses.

[10] 34 U.S.C. §11293(c). The most recent law to reauthorize the Missing Children's Assistance Act (P.L. 113-38) amended the prior law by changing the requirement for OJJDP to conduct incidence studies of missing children from "periodically" to "triennially."

passage in 1984, DOJ has supported three national incidence studies, known as the National Incidence Studies of Missing, Abducted, Runaway, and Thrownaway Children (NISMART- 1, 2, and 3). NISMART-1 was conducted in 1988, NISMART-2 was conducted in 1999, and NISMART-3 was conducted primarily in 2013.

DOJ has issued findings from NISMART-3 in two reports.[11] One of the reports includes findings from a telephone and online survey of households.[12] As with NISMART-2, NISMART-3 includes five categories of missing children:

- abductions by a family member;
- adductions by a nonfamily member perpetrator;
- run away or thrown away children;
- missing because they were lost, stranded, or injured; or
- missing for benign reasons (e.g., misunderstanding about a child's schedule).

The study classifies missing children cases as "caretaker missing" and "reported missing." For an episode to qualify as "caretaker

---

[11] Due to challenges with fielding NISMART-3, DOJ made a competitive award with FY2017 funding to improve data collection of missing children more generally. U.S. Department of Justice (DOJ), Office of Justice Programs (OJP), Office of Juvenile Justice and Delinquency Prevention (OJJDP), Grant Solicitation, *OJJDP FY 2017 National Incidence Studies of Missing Children Reported to Law Enforcement*, 2017, https://www.ojjdp.gov/grants/solicitations/FY2017/NISMCRLE.pdf. DOJ awarded funds to researchers to collect data on child victims of stereotypical kidnappings known to law enforcement agencies and develop and evaluate strategies to collect information from law enforcement agencies about children who are reported missing to them. The funding was awarded to Westat, Inc., a policy research organization, which has partnered with the University of New Hampshire's Crimes Against Children Research Center.

[12] Andrea J. Sedlak, David Finkelhor, and J. Micahel Brick, "National Estimates of Missing Children: Updated Findings From a Survey of Parents and Other Primary Caretakers," *Juvenile Justice Bulletin,* DOJ, OJP, OJJDP June 2017, https://www.ojjdp.gov/pubs/250089.pdf. The report includes definitions of these terms. Some children reported in NISMART-3 were missing, but their caretakers may not have been alarmed or contacted authorities; these children were identified as "non-missing."

missing," the child's whereabouts must have been unknown to the primary caretaker, with the result that the caretaker was alarmed for at least one hour and tried to locate the child. A "caretaker missing" child was considered "reported missing" if a caretaker additionally contacted the police or a missing children's agency to locate the child.

The NISMART-3 household survey indicates that the rates of children who were caretaker missing and reported missing declined since the NISMART-2 study. There was a decrease of 32% for caretaker missing cases (from 9.2 per 1,000 in 1999 to 6.3 per 1,000 in 2013) and a decrease of 52% for reported missing cases (from 6.5 per 1,000 in 1999 to 3.1 per 1,000 in 2013). The drop was largely driven by the decline in the rate of children who were missing due to benign reasons. One of the NISMART-3 reports speculates that the increased use of cell phones has improved communication between parents and their children, and therefore fewer children were perceived or reported as missing. The report raises concerns about the methodological challenges with the survey, including that households were difficult to reach because many now only have cell phones. As a result, the overall sample was smaller than the NISMART-2 sample.

A second NISMART-3 report, which focuses on stereotypical kidnappings, was based on cases known to law enforcement in 2011.[13] Such kidnappings refer to nonfamily abduction in which a slight acquaintance or stranger moves the child at least 20 feet or holds the child at least one hour. In addition to these criteria, the child has to be detained overnight, transported at least 50 miles, held for ransom, abducted with the intent to keep the child permanently, or killed. The report indicates that 105 children were victims of stereotypical kidnappings in 2011.

---

[13] Janis Wolak, David Finkelhor, and Andrea J. Sedlak, "Child Victims of Stereotypical Kidnappings Known to Law Enforcement in 2011," DOJ, OJP, OJJDP, *Juvenile Justice Bulletin,* June 2016, http://www.ojjdp.gov/pubs/249249.pdf.

Sexually Exploited Children

The true number of sexual exploitation incidents—whether they accompany missing children cases or not—is unknown because this type of abuse often goes undetected. In addition, studies of child sexual exploitation report varying numbers because of differences in their methodology, the time periods over which the data were collected, and how exploitation is defined. Nonetheless, one federal study, the National Survey of Children's Exposure to Violence, provides some insight into the prevalence of sexual exploitation. The study shows that a significant number and share of children under age 18 have been sexually victimized.

The National Survey of Children's Exposure to Violence, conducted by the University of New Hampshire with support from OJJDP, examined the incidence and prevalence of children's exposure to violence in 2008.[14] Researchers interviewed a nationally representative sample of children under age 18 and their caretakers by phone. They asked whether children had experienced certain forms of violence and victimization, including sexual victimization, within the past year and over their lifetime. The sexual victimization category encompasses seven types of victimization: sexual conduct or fondling by an adult the child knew, sexual conduct or fondling by an adult stranger, sexual contact or fondling by another child or teenager, attempted or completed intercourse, exposure or "flashing," sexual harassment, and consensual sexual conduct with an adult. The study found that 1 in 16 (6.1%) surveyed children and youth were sexually victimized in the past year and nearly 1 in 10 (9.8%) were sexually

---

[14] David Finkelhor et al., *Children's Exposure to Violence: A Comprehensive National Survey*, DOJ, OJP, OJJDP, October 2009, http://www.ncjrs.gov/pdffiles1/ojjdp/227744.pdf.

victimized at some point over their lifetimes. Girls were more likely than boys to report that they had been sexually victimized, with 7.4% of girls reporting sexual victimization within the past year and 12.2% reporting victimization over their lifetimes. Female adolescents ages 14 to 17 had the highest rate of victimization. Nearly 8% had been sexually victimized within the past year and 18.7% had been sexually victimized over their lifetimes.

FUNDING FOR THE MEC PROGRAM

The MEC program was initially funded at $4 million in FY1985 and has received funding increases in most years since 1991. Funding more than doubled from $6.0 million in FY1997 to $12.3 million in FY1998, when the ICAC Task Force program was implemented. Another funding peak, from FY2003 to FY2004, was the result of increased funds for the AMBER Alert program and NCMEC.

Funding increased again—from $50 million in FY2008 to $70 million in FY2009—following reauthorization of the program. Also in FY2009, Congress appropriated funding for the program under the American Recovery and Reinvestment Act (ARRA, P.L. 111-5). ARRA provided funding for myriad federal programs and initiatives to address the economic recession that began in December 2007 and extended through June 2009. Specifically, the law appropriated $50 million for the ICAC Task Force program.

Table 1 shows total funding and funding for each of the program's components from FY2006 through FY2017. NCMEC has received the most funding in each of these years, followed by the ICAC Task Force program. The next highest level of funding support went to activities including program administration, training and technical assistance on missing and exploited children, support services for missing children's organizations, and grant programs that can vary from year to year.

The FY2017 appropriation for the MEC program was $72.5 million. As with prior appropriations legislation, the FY2017 appropriations law (P.L. 115-31) did not specify the level of funds for each of the program's components. DOJ allocated $63.1 million for the program, with the remaining $9.3 million allocated for other expenses within the OJP and OJJDP programs; approximately $58,000 was not obligated.[15]

NATIONAL CENTER FOR MISSING AND EXPLOITED CHILDREN

NCMEC is a primary component of the MEC program and employs more than 300 people at its Alexandria, VA, headquarters and regional offices in California, Florida, New York, and Texas. These regional offices provide case management and technical support in their geographic areas.

NCMEC provides multiple activities and services pertaining to

- missing children, including those abducted to or from the United States;
- exploited children;
- training and technical assistance;
- families of missing children; and
- partnerships with state missing children's clearinghouses and other stakeholders.

---

[15] Based on CRS correspondence with DOJ, OJP, December 2017.

Table 1. Actual Funding for the Missing and Exploited Children's Program, by Component, FY2006-FY2017

(In thousands of dollars)

Program Component	FY2006	FY2007	FY2008	FY2009	FY2010	FY2011	FY2012	FY2013	FY2014	FY2015	FY2016	FY2017
NCMEC	$26,259	$26,500	$24,740	$30,488	$30,496	$30,130	$26,623	$25,500	$26,005	$25,700	$28,343	$28,343
ICAC Task Force Program	$14,133	$11,779[a]	$15,950	$25,000[b]	$28,800[b]	$28,583	$25,670	$25,050	$27,049	$27,049	$27,600	$27,600
AMBER Alert Training and	$4,936	$5,000	$4,481	$5,000	$3,150	$4,075	$2,515	$2,364	N/A[c]	$2,402	$2,400	$2,400
Technical Assistance												
Grant Programs and	$2,059	$4,108	$4,829	$9,512	$7,554	$7,072	$10,192	$9,478	$7,270	$5,865	$4,194	$4,231
Technical Assistance[d]												
Total Funding	*$47,387*	*$47,387*	*$50,000*	*$70,000*	*$70,000*	*$69,860*	*$65,000*	*$62,392*	*$60,324*	*$61,016*	*$62,536*	*$63,124*

Sources: Congressional Research Service, based on information provided by the U.S. Department of Justice, Office of Justice Programs, March, July, and October 2014; October 2015; October 2016; and November 2017; Continuing and Further Continuing Appropriations Act, 2013 (P.L. 113-6); Rules Committee Print 113-32 on the amendment to H.R. 3547, which was enacted as P.L. 113-67; Consolidated and Further Continuing Appropriations Act, 2015 (P.L. 113-235); Consolidated Appropriations Act, 2016 (P.L. 114-113); Consolidated Appropriations Act, 2017 (P.L. 115-31); and correspondence with the U.S. Department of Justice, Office of Justice Programs, Office of Communications, October 2015, October 2016, and December 2017. Appropriations reflect rescissions where applicable, and the FY2013 appropriations reflect amounts post-sequestration as required under the terms of the Budget Control Act of 2011 (P.L. 112-25) and the Balanced Budget and Emergency Deficit Control Act of 1985 (P.L. 99-177), as amended.

Notes: In most years, some funding is reprogrammed to support activities under the Office of Justice Programs (OJP) and the Office of Juvenile Justice and Delinquency Prevention (OJJDP). In addition, some funding (generally between $1 and $60,000) is unobligated. For example, the FY2017 appropriation for the MEC program was $72,500,000. Of this amount, $63,124,000 was allocated to the components of the program; $7,091,479 was reprogrammed for other OJP activities; and $2,227,026 was used to support OJJDP functions (i.e., website, communication functions, training and technical assistance standards, and performance measures). Another $57,652 was unobligated.

[a] The ICAC Task Force program received an additional $11.5 million in 2007 through the Byrne Discretionary Grant Program to expand the program, provide training and technical assistance, and improve the forensic capabilities of task forces and reduce the backlog of cases they handle. These funds are not included in this table.

[b] The ICAC received $50 million under the American Recovery and Reinvestment Act (ARRA, P.L. 111-5) to support four ICAC activities authorized under the PROTECT Our Children Act of 2008 (P.L. 110-401): (1) ICAC grants; (2) ICAC Training and Technical Assistance grant; (3) ICAC Research grants to encourage innovative and independent research and data collection to further understand the scope and prevalence of technology and Internet crimes against children; and (4) the National ICAC Data System. These funds are not included in this table.

[c] Remaining funds from previous years were carried over to support AMBER Alert activities through FY2014.

[d] This includes funding for program administration, support services for missing children's organizations, and grant programs that can vary from year to year.

These activities and services are detailed further in this section.[16] Note that some missing children and exploited children programs are not mutually exclusive, and this report does not provide an exhaustive discussion of all services provided by NCMEC.[17] In addition to funding through the MEC program, NCMEC is also funded through private contributions, other DOJ grants, and the United States Secret Service (USSS) in the Department of Homeland Security (DHS). Pursuant to the Violent Crime Control and Law Enforcement Act of 1994 (P.L. 103-322), Congress has mandated that the USSS provide forensic and technical assistance to NCMEC and federal, state, and local law enforcement agencies in matters involving missing and exploited children. In recent years, funding provided by the USSS has been transferred to OJP to be provided directly to NCMEC.

Missing Children's Services

Call Center

NCMEC's Call Center receives calls on its 24-hour toll-free hotline (1-800-THE-LOST), primarily from parents and law enforcement officials. In FY2017, the center responded to over 224,600 calls reporting missing children; sightings of missing children; and requests for assistance, information, and technical assistance from families of missing children, law enforcement agencies, and others.[18] Since 1987,

---

[16] Unless otherwise noted, the description of these services is based on a site visit to NCMEC, interviews and ongoing correspondence with NCMEC staff, and quarterly progress reports submitted by NCMEC to the Department of Justice about the status of the grant received under the Missing and Exploited Children's program.

[17] For further information about NCMEC, see its website: http://www.missingkids.org/.

[18] Based on correspondence with the National Center for Missing and Exploited Children, December 2017.

reports of child sexual exploitation received through the CyberTipline are routed to the Call Center. Assistance activities range from sending publications or educational materials to providing technical support to law enforcement and families about missing children cases. The Call Center also provides information to families of missing children about free or low-cost transportation services or requests transportation for families needing assistance with reunification.

NCMEC is the only nonprofit, non-law enforcement entity to have access to the FBI's National Crime Information Center (NCIC) Missing Person File, which is reviewed by Call Center staff for records of missing children added by local and state law enforcement agencies and updates of these records. Law enforcement agencies submitting information to NCIC on a missing child are to notify NCMEC of each report that relates to a child reportedly missing from foster care, and they must maintain close liaison with NCMEC (and child welfare agencies) to exchange information and technical assistance about missing children cases generally.[19] Cases of children who are believed to be seriously at risk are flagged in NCIC for NCMEC. NCMEC is permitted to search the Missing Person File to assist with long-term missing children who would be over age 18.

Case Management

Each missing child case is entered into NCMEC's nationwide database, and a case manager in the Missing Children's Division is assigned. NCMEC case managers serve as the single point of contact for the searching family and provide technical assistance to locate abductors and recover missing children. In FY2017, case managers handled 26,956 cases (i.e., individual children). Of these, about 9 out of 10 involved runaways.[20]

---

[19] 34 U.S.C. §41308.

[20] Based on correspondence with the National Center for Missing and Exploited Children, December 2017.

Project ALERT (America's Law Enforcement Retiree Team) and Team Adam

The Project ALERT program was established in 1992 to assist law enforcement agencies with the recovery of missing children—particularly long-term cases—at no cost to the agencies. Project ALERT members include approximately 150 retired federal, state, and local law enforcement officials who have recent and relevant investigative experience.[21] Project ALERT services include case review, organization, recommendation of investigative strategies, assistance with case interviews, and liaison efforts with the family of a missing child. Representatives also conduct outreach to the community through public speaking and attending conferences.

Team Adam, created in 2003, is designed to be a rapid, onsite response and support system that provides investigative and technical assistance to local law enforcement agencies at no cost to them. The team is staffed by approximately 90 retired federal, state, and local investigators, and is chosen by a committee with representatives from the FBI and state and local law enforcement executives experienced in crimes-against-children investigations.[22] Team Adam consultants determine the additional resources or assistance that would assist in the search for the victim, the investigation of the crime, and family crisis management.

Forensic Services Unit

The Forensic Services Unit is composed of the Forensic Imaging Unit and a Biometrics Team. The teams assist in the recovery of long-term missing children and work to identify the remains of deceased children and young adults believed to have gone missing. The Forensic

[21] NCMEC, NCMEC Quarterly Progress Reports, July 1 – Sept. 30, 2017, p. 15.
[22] Ibid., p. 18.

Imaging Unit was created in 1990 to "age-progress" images of missing children through software programs using the most recent picture of the child. The image is stretched to approximate normal cranial and facial growth, and the resultant image is merged and blended with a photograph of an immediate biological family member.[23] The age-progressed image appears in clothing and with a hairstyle consistent with the child's current age. Missing children photos are age-progressed every two years, and adult photos are age-progressed in five-year increments. Age-progressed images are distributed to the local police, searching families, and media, and posted on the NCMEC website. The Forensic Unit also creates age-regressed images. These are produced at the request of law enforcement agents posing as youth in online communication with adults who seek to engage in sexual acts with children.

Staff in the Biometric Team provide support and resources for long-term missing child cases and cases of unidentified human remains of victims believed to be children and young adults. They assist law enforcement and medical examiners/coroners in identifying unknown children, either deceased or living, by facilitating the collection of DNA, dental information, fingerprints, facial reconstructions, photo enhancements, and documentation of personal belongings found with the child. Once collected, the information is uploaded to the National Missing and Unidentified Persons System (NamUs), so it can be compared directly against the information collected from unidentified persons.[24] NamUs is a program created by OJP to serve as a central repository and resource center for missing persons and unidentified decedent records. It contains databases storing detailed information about missing people and unidentified remains and may be searched for possible matches among cases.[25]

---

[23] Based on congressional briefing by NCMEC staff, August 27, 2013.

[24] NCMEC, *NCMEC Quarterly Progress Reports, July 1 to Sept. 30, 2017*, p. 14.

[25] DOJ, OJP, NamUs: National Institute of Justice, National Missing and Unidentified Persons Systems, http://www.namus.gov/.

International Missing Children's Cases

NCMEC assists with cases of children abducted to and from the United States.[26] From 1995 through May 2008, NCMEC had a Cooperative Agreement with the State Department and OJJDP to handle *incoming* cases of international abduction to the United States under The Hague Convention on the Civil Aspects of International Child Abduction (the "Hague Convention").[27] The State Department is now responsible for handling these cases. NCMEC assists the State Department with developing and distributing posters for missing children. Signatories to the Hague Convention pledge to work toward the prompt return of abducted children. Of the 195 officially recognized countries in the world, however, 120 do not have formal civil mechanisms in place with the United States to facilitate the return of a parentally abducted child.[28]

NCMEC also coordinates cases of American children abducted abroad, or *outgoing* cases. NCMEC provides technical assistance to law enforcement in support of federal statute that criminalizes removing a child from the United States "with the intent to obstruct the lawful exercise of parental rights."[29]

NCMEC handles hundreds of prevention and abduction-in-progress matters each year that involve international abduction. It also coordinates the provision of pro-bono legal assistance to victim families

---

[26] The International Centre for Missing and Exploited Children ("ICMEC") is a sister organization affiliated with NCMEC. ICMEC focuses on policy, advocacy, and training, and does not perform case work. ICMEC advocates for adoption of treaties in regard to children's rights; engages international law enforcement officials, civil service organizations, and government representatives; offers technical assistance in creating missing children centers; and creates and distributes reports on international child abduction and child sexual exploitation.

[27] The Department of State is designated as the U.S. Central Authority for the Hague Convention. NCMEC was permitted to serve as the representative of the State Department pursuant to 42 U.S.C. §11608.

[28] NCMEC, *NCMEC Quarterly Progress Report: July 1-September 30, 2017,* p. 56, footnote 58.

[29] 18 U.S.C. §1204(a). The term parental rights refers to the right to joint or sole physical custody of a child obtained through a court order, a legally binding agreement between the involved parties, or operation of law. For further information about the International Parental Kidnapping Crime Act and the Hague Convention, see CRS Report RS21261, *International Parental Child Abductions*, by Alison M. Smith.

and provides technical support, including legal technical assistance to parents, lawyers, court officers, law enforcement officials, and others.

Response to Child Sexual Exploitation

Pursuant to the Violent Crime Control and Law Enforcement Act of 1994 (P.L. 103-322), Congress mandated that the United States Secret Service provide forensic and technical assistance to NCMEC and federal, state, and local law enforcement agencies in matters involving missing and exploited children. NCMEC's Exploited Children's Division (ECD) was established in January 1997 with a grant from USSS received pursuant to P.L. 103-322. The USSS continues to provide funding for this purpose.

The ECD administers the Child Victim ID Program (CVIP) and CyberTipline. The unit also analyzes data and forwards requests to appropriate NCMEC divisions and departments and monitors online services, news reports, and other sources each day for new cases and information relative to the issues of child sexual exploitation. The ECD follows up with law enforcement agencies about cases of exploited children. In addition to the ECD, two separate units in NCMEC—the Sex Offender Tracking Team and the Child Sex Trafficking Team within the Case Analysis Division—also work on exploited children's issues.

The Child Victim Identification Program (CVIP)

CVIP formally began in 2002 in response to the decision in *Ashcroft v. Free Speech Coalition* (2002), in which the Supreme Court held that federal laws prohibiting pornography are enforceable when they involve identified children, not images that appear to be children.[30] CVIP analysts assist law enforcement officers and prosecutors with

[30] Ashcroft v. Free Speech Coalition, 535 U.S. 234 (2002).

child pornography cases throughout the country using their knowledge of child pornography series and relevant computer software. Law enforcement agencies may submit seized images to federal law enforcement agents detailed to NCMEC and request that CVIP examine the images. CVIP analysts use computer software and visual analysis to determine whether any of the images contain identified child victims. In addition, NCMEC has a secure website (the Victim Identification Lab) for law enforcement officers, prosecutors, and social service workers to examine sanitized images that contain clues about a child's whereabouts. Authorized users can examine the images and post comments and suggestions for both NCMEC and other authorized users.

CyberTipline

The CyberTipline, created in March 1998, serves as the national clearinghouse for tips and leads about child sexual exploitation, and is available 24 hours a day, seven days a week. The tipline allows the public to report online incidents involving child sexual exploitation, and electronic communication services or remote computing service providers (collectively known as electronic service providers or ESPs) are required by law to report such incidents.[31] Although the CyberTipline began operating in 1998, NCMEC's role as its administrator was formally authorized by the Prosecutorial Remedies and Other Tools to End the Exploitation of Children Today (PROTECT) Act of 2003 (P.L. 108-21). The authorizing statute for the

[31] 34 U.S.C. §11293(b)(1)(P). The tipline enables ESPs and members of the public to report under eight categories: (1) possession, manufacture, and distribution of child pornography; (2) online enticement of children for sexual acts; (3) child sex trafficking, including child prostitution; (4) child sex tourism; (5) child sexual molestation (not in the family); (6) unsolicited obscene material sent to a child; (7) misleading domain names; and (8) misleading words or digital images on the Internet. The first three reporting categories were specified in P.L. 108-21, and the other five categories were specified in the Protecting Our Children Comes First Act of 2007 (P.L. 110-240). The Justice for Victims of Trafficking Act (P.L. 114-22) struck "child prostitution" and replaced it with "child sex trafficking, including child prostitution."

MEC program states that the CyberTipline is intended to take reports of "Internet-related child sexual exploitation," but in practice, such incidents do not have to be facilitated by the Internet. After evaluating the reports and rating them based on risk to the child, NCMEC makes reports to the CyberTipline (along with accompanying analysis) available to select federal, state, and local law enforcement agencies through a secure web-based system.[32]

Sex Offender Tracking Team

The Adam Walsh Child Protection and Safety Act of 2006 (P.L. 109-248) expanded the requirements for state law enforcement and prison officials to track and register sex offenders. NCMEC's Sex Offender Tracking Team, in its Case Analysis Division, provides assistance to federal, state, and local law enforcement in their efforts to locate and apprehend noncompliant sex offenders by providing technical assistance and analysis. The team developed a standard protocol in response to law enforcement requests for assistance in locating fugitive sex offenders, which generally includes information obtained through public databases and search tools routinely used by NCMEC analysts. The team participates in the National Sex Offender Targeting Center, an interagency intelligence and operations center created by the U.S. Marshals Service.

Child Sex Trafficking Team

The Child Sex Trafficking Team compares reports of suspected child sex trafficking victims submitted to the CyberTipline with reports of missing children received by the Missing Children's Division. It also provides technical support and analysis to the FBI's Innocence Lost National Initiative. The team provides technical assistance to law

---

[32] U.S. Government Accountability Office, Combating Child Pornography: Steps are Needed to Ensure That Tips to Law Enforcement are Useful and Forensic Examinations are Cost Effective, GAO-11-334, March 2011, p. 9, http://www.gao.gov/new.items/d11334.pdf. (Hereinafter, U.S. Government Accountability Office, Combating Child Pornography.)

enforcement agencies working to identify and recover children in the United States who have been victimized by sex trafficking, including those involved in the FBI's Innocence Lost National Initiative. Analysts in the unit provide reports about offenders who sexually exploited children through sex trafficking, and they provide information to law enforcement officials about known missing child cases possibly linked to sex trafficking.[33]

Family Advocacy Services

NCMEC's Family Advocacy Division provides support, crisis intervention, and technical assistance to families, law enforcement, and family-advocacy agencies. Team HOPE (Help Offering Parents Empowerment), a component of the division, consists of trained volunteers who have experienced the disappearance of a child in their family. These volunteers mentor other parents and families of missing children to help them cope during and after the incident.

Training and Technical Assistance

NCMEC trainers provide on- and offsite training and technical assistance to law enforcement, criminal and juvenile justice professionals, and healthcare professionals nationwide and in Canada. Training involves issues relating to child sexual exploitation and missing-child case detection, identification of victims, investigation, prevention, and forensic imaging. NCMEC provides nationally accredited training about infant security for healthcare professionals and law enforcement.

---

[33] NCMEC, "Child Sex Trafficking," http://www.missingkids.com/CSTT.

Partnerships

NCMEC works closely with federal agencies, some of which have detailed agents and analysts to work at NCMEC part-time or full-time. These analysts follow CyberTipline leads and work with NCMEC to develop policy and procedures around children missing internationally, among other activities.

NCMEC also works with missing children's clearinghouses in each state, the District of Columbia, Puerto Rico, the U.S. Virgin Islands, and Canada.[34] These clearinghouses disseminate information and collect data about missing individuals, provide technical assistance in cases of missing and exploited children, and network with other clearinghouses. NCMEC provides the clearinghouses with training, technical assistance, and information to assist them in handling missing-children cases.

Further, NCMEC serves as the national clearinghouse for AMBER Alert information about abducted children and their perpetrators, and employs a full-time AMBER Alert law enforcement liaison. (See "AMBER Alert Program" for more information.) NCMEC verifies AMBER Alerts and disseminates information about an abduction to authorized secondary distributors that can target messages to their customers in a specific geographic region. Only law enforcement can initiate and release AMBER Alerts for primary distribution.[35]

In 2006, NCMEC and the International Centre for Missing and Exploited Children joined with 34 international financial institutions and Internet industry leaders to combat commercial online child pornography.[36] The purpose of the coalition is to prevent the purchase and sale of child pornography over the Internet and to engage in

---

[34] For further information, see NCMEC, *Missing Child Clearinghouses*, http://www.missingkids.com/Clearinghouses.

[35] DOJ, OJP, OJJDP, *Report to the Congress on AMBER Alert*, July 2005, p. 7, http://www.amberalert.gov/newsroom/ pdfs/05_amber_report.pdf.

[36] NCMEC, "Financial Coalition Against Child Pornography," http://www.missingkids.com/FCACP.

prevention efforts. NCMEC, law enforcement agencies, and financial institutions share information pertaining to commercial child pornography websites, with the goal of eliminating the ability of users to pay for access to them.

Internet Crimes Against Children (ICAC) Task Force

ICAC Task Forces[37]

The ICAC Task Force program is authorized under the PROTECT Our Children Act of 2008 (P.L. 110-401), as amended. The program supports state and local law enforcement task forces in responding to online enticement of children by sexual perpetrators, child exploitation, and child obscenity and pornography cases. The program serves multiple purposes, including

- increasing the capabilities of state and local law enforcement officers to detect Internet crimes against children and apprehend offenders;
- conducting proactive and reactive Internet crimes against children investigations;
- providing training and technical assistance to ICAC task forces and other law enforcement agencies in the areas of investigation, forensics, prosecution, community outreach, and capacity-building, using recognized experts to assist in the development and delivery of training programs;
- increasing the number of Internet crimes against children offenses being investigated and prosecuted; and

[37] 34 U.S.C. §§21112 et seq.

- delivering Internet crimes against children public awareness and prevention programs.

An ICAC task force is formed when a state or local law enforcement agency enters into a grant contract with OJJDP, and then into a memorandum of understanding with other federal, state, and local agencies. Currently, 61 regional task forces are in operation, each of which is composed of multiple affiliated organizations (most of which are city and county law enforcement agencies).[38] The task forces receive leads from CyberTipline analysts at NCMEC and concerned citizens or develop leads through proactive investigations and undercover operations. The Attorney General is to award grants to state and local ICAC task forces using a formula established by DOJ to distribute 75% of the funds; the remaining 25% is to be distributed based on need.

In establishing any formula, DOJ must ensure that each state or local ICAC receives at least 0.5% of the funds available. In addition, DOJ is to take into consideration factors such as each state's population; the number of investigative leads within the task force's jurisdiction; the number of criminal cases related to Internet crimes against children referred to a task force for federal, state, or local prosecution; the number of successful prosecutions of child exploitation cases by a task force; the amount of training, technical assistance, and public education or outreach conducted by a task force on child exploitation offenses; and other criteria established by DOJ to demonstrate the level of need for additional resources.

Pursuant to the law, DOJ established the ICAC Training and Technical Assistance program to provide assistance to ICAC task forces. Multiple entities have been awarded funds to provide training on improving investigation, technologies, and prosecutorial capabilities.[39]

---

[38] DOJ, OJP, OJJDP, "Program Summary: Internet Crimes Against Children Task Program," http://www.ojjdp.gov/ programs/progsummary.asp?pi=3.

[39] Ibid.

National ICAC Data System (NIDS)

The authorizing law for ICAC directs the Attorney General to establish the National ICAC Data System (NIDS).[40] As discussed in the law, the intent of Congress in authorizing the data system was to build upon Operation Fairplay, developed by the Wyoming Attorney General's office. Operation Fairplay established a secure, undercover infrastructure that has facilitated online law enforcement investigations of child exploitation, information sharing, and the capacity to collect and aggregate data on the extent of the problem of child exploitation.[41]

The law specified that the system is to be housed and maintained within DOJ or a credentialed law enforcement agency and is to be available for a nominal charge to support law enforcement agencies' efforts to combat child exploitation. It must also collect and report real-time data; provide an undercover infrastructure for users; identify high-priority suspects; and include a network that provides for secure, online data storage and analysis, among other items.

DOJ issued a grant solicitation in March 2009 for constructing, maintaining, and housing NIDS; however, grant applicants were notified in January 2010 that DOJ would not make an award under that solicitation and instead would pursue a different system for "deconfliction" and investigation than was described in the solicitation.[42] DOJ issued another solicitation in June 2010 to select a

---

[40] 34 U.S.C. §21115.

[41] DOJ, *The National Strategy for Child Exploitation Prevention and Interdiction: A Report to Congress*, August 2010, pp. 10-12, http://www.justice.gov/psc/docs/natstrategyreport.pdf. (Hereinafter, DOJ, *The National Strategy for Child Exploitation Prevention and Interdiction: A Report to Congress*.)

[42] Deconfliction is the coordination and information sharing among law enforcement agencies on multi-jurisdiction investigations to help ensure officer safety and the effective use of resources. U.S. Government Accountability Office (GAO), *Combating Child Pornography*, GAO-11-334, March 2011.

grantee to conduct a national needs assessment and perform other tasks to support the future development of NIDS.[43]

In September 2011, DOJ awarded funds to the West Virginia State Police to develop and implement the ICAC Deconfliction System (IDS), which was launched in December 2014. It is used by all ICAC task forces and other registered law enforcement users. IDS enables users to contribute and access data (e.g., name, alias, email address, IP address of perpetrator and related information) to resolve case conflicts. Information about a potential perpetrator is compared against other databases that store information about crimes committed against children. IDS alerts the user if information has been collected on the potential perpetrator in these other systems, and informs the user of other law enforcement agencies working on a case involving the perpetrator.[44]

National Strategy for Child Exploitation Prevention and Interdiction

The ICAC authorizing law directs the Attorney General to create and implement a National Strategy for Child Exploitation Prevention and Interdiction.[45] The law specifies that the strategy is to involve

---

[43] DOJ OJP, OJJDP, *Needs Assessment and Development Activities for the National Internet Crimes Against Children Data System (NIDS)*, no date, http://www.ojjdp.gov/grants/solicitations/FY2010/ARRA%20NIDS.pdf. In September 2010, OJJDP awarded a grant to the Massachusetts State Police (MASP) and its partners to conduct a national needs assessment for NIDS. According to DOJ, work on and payment for the grant were suspended due to misconduct involving a former MASP employee who was investigated by DOJ's Office of the Inspector General. P.L. 112-206 required DOJ to submit a report to Congress about the status of the data system. See DOJ, OJP, OJJDP, *Report on the National Internet Crimes Against Children Data System (NIDS) Project, Pursuant to the Child Protection Act of 2012 (*P.L. 112-206*)*, no date.

[44] DOJ, OJP, OJJDP, *Internet Crimes Against Children Data System*, fact sheet, no date; and CRS correspondence with DOJ, OJP, October 2015.

[45] 34 U.S.C. §2111. The law additionally directed the Department of Justice to appoint a senior official to serve as coordinator of the national strategy. DOJ appointed the National Coordinator in January 2010. Soon thereafter, the national coordinator convened the National Strategy Working Group to assist in implementing the national strategy. See U.S.

establishing long-range, comprehensive goals concerning child exploitation and that DOJ is to coordinate its programs to combat child exploitation with other federal programs, as well as with international, state, local, and tribal law enforcement agencies and the private sector. As part of this strategy, DOJ is directed to assess the ICAC program, including an evaluation of how entities that comprise each task force coordinate on investigations, and the success of task forces in leveraging state and local resources and matching funds. The law also directs the Attorney General to conduct periodic reviews of the effectiveness of each ICAC task force, and to submit a report on the strategy to Congress every other year. Two reports have been issued, one in August 2010 and another in April 2016. Both reports discuss the ICAC Task Force program, an assessment of threats to children, and the work of federal agencies to combat child sexual exploitation.[46]

AMBER ALERT PROGRAM

AMBER (America's Missing: Broadcast Emergency Response) Alert systems are state-administered communication systems to inform the public about children who are abducted. AMBER systems are voluntary partnerships—between law enforcement agencies, broadcasters, and transportation agencies—to activate messages in a targeted area when a child is abducted and believed to be in grave

Government Accountability Office (GAO), *Combating Child Pornography*, GAO-11-334, March 2011, pp. 12-13.

[46] DOJ, The National Strategy for Child Exploitation Prevention and Interdiction: A Report to Congress, August 2010; and DOJ, The National Strategy for Child Exploitation and Prevention: A Report to Congress, April 2016, https://www.justice.gov/psc/file/842411/download. The first report identified the following types of child sexual exploitation: (1) child pornography, (2) online enticement of children for sexual purposes, (3) commercial sexual exploitation of children (primarily domestic prostitution), and (4) child sex tourism. The second report identified five types of child sexual exploitation: (1) child pornography, (2) sextortion and live streaming of child sexual abuse, (3) child sex trafficking, (4) child sex tourism, and (5) sex offender registry violations.

danger. The first system began locally in 1996 when fourth-grader Amber Hagerman was abducted and murdered near her home in the Dallas-Fort Worth area. After the abduction, law enforcement agencies in North Texas and the Dallas-Fort Worth Association of Radio Managers developed a plan to send out an emergency alert about a missing child to the public through the Emergency Alert System (EAS), which interrupts broadcasting.[47] Soon after, jurisdictions in Texas and other states began to create regional alert programs.

OJP first provided funding ($10 million in discretionary appropriations) in 2002 for states and localities to develop AMBER Alert programs. The PROTECT Act (P.L. 108-21), enacted in 2003, directed the Attorney General to create a national AMBER Alert program, including appointing a coordinator and developing standards for issuing an alert.[48] P.L. 108-21 also authorized funding for activities to support states in developing AMBER Alert communication plans and technologies.

AMBER Alert Coordinator and Standards

P.L. 108-21 provided that the Attorney General appoint an AMBER Alert coordinator to (1) work with states to encourage the development of additional regional and local AMBER Alert plans;

2. serve as the regional coordinator for abducted children throughout the AMBER Alert network;
3. create voluntary standards for the issuance of alerts, including minimum standards that address the special needs of the child (such as health care needs), and limit the alerts to a geographic area most likely to facilitate the abduction of the child, without

[47] For further discussion about the distribution of the alerts, see archived CRS Report RS21453, *Amber Alert Program Technology*.

[48] 34 U.S.C. §20501.

interfering with the current system of voluntary coordination between local broadcasters and law enforcement;

4. submit a report to Congress by March 1, 2005, on the activities of the coordinator and the effectiveness and status of the AMBER plans of each state that has implemented one; and (5) consult with the FBI and cooperate with the Federal Communications Commission in implementing the program.

In 2003, the DOJ AMBER Alert coordinator was appointed. The coordinator convened a national advisory group to oversee the national initiative and make recommendations on the AMBER Alert criteria, examine new technologies, identify best practices, and identify issues with implementation. On the basis of the group's recommendations, the department issued guidelines for issuing an alert:

- law enforcement officials have a reasonable belief that an abduction has occurred,
- law enforcement officials believe that the child is in imminent danger of serious bodily injury or death,
- enough descriptive information exists about the victim and the abductor for law enforcement to issue an alert,
- the victim is age 17 or younger, and
- the child's name and other critical data elements have been entered into the NCIC.

A new AMBER Alert "flag" was created within the NCIC's Missing Person File for abducted children for whom an alert has been issued. DOJ submitted a report to Congress in 2005 that provided an overview of its strategy to facilitate a national AMBER Alert plan and the criteria developed for issuing an alert.[49]

---

[49] DOJ, OJP, OJJDP, Report to the Congress on AMBER Alert.

AMBER Alert Grant Programs

P.L. 108-21 provides three authorizations to support states in implementing AMBER Alert communication plans and technologies: (1) an authorization of $4 million in FY2004 to DOJ for grants to states to develop and implement AMBER Alert communication programs, which allows states to pursue activities specified in the law; (2) an additional $5 million in FY2004 to DOJ to provide funding to states to develop and implement new technologies to improve Amber Alert communications; and (3) $20 million to the Department of Transportation (DOT) in FY2004 for grants to states to develop and enhance notification or communication systems along highways.

With regard to the DOJ authorization, the law specifies that the department is to provide grants to states, on a geographically equitable basis if possible, for developing and enhancing their AMBER Alert communications plans. The federal government is to provide no more than 50% of the costs for carrying out the activities specified in the law related to communication plans. DOJ determined that funds would be most efficiently spent providing training and technical assistance to law enforcement and state officials on abducted children, including providing assessments of AMBER Alert communication plans.[50] This is instead of funding that is awarded to states to implement communication plans, including the more narrow activity of developing and implementing new technologies. Every five years, OJJDP issues a competitive solicitation seeking bids to provide technical assistance, and it has awarded funding under this solicitation to Fox Valley Technical College in Wisconsin.[51]

---

[50] This information was provided to the Congressional Research Service by DOJ, OJP in May 2007 and updated in December 2017.

[51] DOJ, "AMBER Alert Program, Technical Assistance," http://www.amber-net.org/technical assistance.html.

As noted, P.L. 108-21 authorized $20 million in FY2004 for DOT to fund states in developing and enhancing communications systems along highways for alerts and other information to assist in the recovery of abducted children. States are eligible to receive funding (up to $400,000 each) to be used for the *implementation* of a communications program that employs changeable message signs or other motorist information systems—if DOT determines that the state has already developed the program.[52] The federal share of the cost of these activities is not to exceed 80%, and federal funds are available until expended.[53] As of the end of FY2017 (September 30, 2016), 40 states and the District of Columbia had received funding, and approximately $3.1 million was still available.

GRANT PROGRAMS AND TECHNICAL ASSISTANCE

The MEC program provides funding to support other activities related to missing and exploited children, including training and technical assistance for public and private nonprofit organizations.[54] OJJDP contracts with Fox Valley Technical College in Wisconsin to provide technical assistance, which focuses on strengthening multi-disciplinary responses in child victimization cases. Assistance is

---

[52] Pursuant to the PROTECT Act, states are eligible to receive two types of DOT grants. *Development* grants to be used to develop general policies, procedures, training, and communication systems for changeable message signs or other motorist information about an abduction. *Implementation* grants are to be used to support the infrastructure of the program. Funding authorized under the PROTECT Act was used exclusively for the implementation of communication systems to issue AMBER alerts. However, states are eligible to apply for grants of up to $125,000 each, through a separate DOT appropriation for the Intelligent Transportation Systems program, to support state departments of transportation efforts related to AMBER Alert planning. These funds are available until expended.

[53] This information was provided to the Congressional Research Service by the Department of Transportation, Federal Highway Administration, December 2017.

[54] For further information, see DOJ, OJP, OJJDP, "Missing and Exploited Children's Program Training and Technical Assistance," http://mecptraining.org/; and Fox Valley Technical College, "Missing and Exploited Children," https://ncjtc.fvtc.edu/programs/PR00000004/missing-and-exploited-children.

provided through distance learning, webinars, onsite technical assistance, or classroom formats.

APPENDIX. THE MISSING CHILDREN'S ASSISTANCE ACT OF 1984, AS AMENDED

Table A-1. The Missing Children's Assistance Act of 1984 and Amendments to the Act

Year (Public Law)	Description
1984 (P.L. 98-473)	—Defines missing child as any individual under age 18 whose whereabouts are unknown to such individual's legal custodian if he or she was removed from control of his or her legal custodian without custodian's consent or the circumstances strongly indicate that such individual is likely to be abused or sexually exploited; —Directs the Administrator of the Office of Juvenile Justice and Delinquency Prevention (OJJDP) to (1) facilitate effective coordination among all federally funded programs relating to missing children, (2) establish and operate a national toll-free telephone line for individuals to report information regarding the location of any missing child, or other child 13 years old or younger whose whereabouts are unknown, (3) establish and operate a national resource center and clearinghouse designed to provide technical assistance to state and local governments and law enforcement agencies, disseminate information about innovative and model missing children's programs, and periodically conduct national incidence studies to determine the number of missing children, (4) analyze, compile, publish, and disseminate an annual summary of recently completed research relating to missing children with emphasis on effective models of inter-governmental coordination and effective programs designed to promote community awareness of missing children, among others, and (5) prepare an annual comprehensive plan for facilitating cooperation and coordination among all agencies and organizations with responsibilities related to missing children; —Authorizes the OJJDP Administrator to make grants and enter into contracts for research, demonstration projects, or service programs designed to disseminate information about missing children, locate missing children, and collect information from states or localities on the investigative practices used by law enforcement agencies in missing children's cases, among other purposes; and —Provides funding authorization at $10 million for FY1985 and such sums as necessary forFY1986 through FY1988.

Table A-1. (Continued)

Year (Public Law)	Description
1988 (P.L. 100-690)	—Removes the requirement that the OJJDP Administrator analyze, compile, publish, and disseminate an annual summary of recently completed research concerning missing and exploited children; —Requires the OJJDP Administrator to submit a report, within 180 days after the end of each fiscal year, to the President and Congress, including a comprehensive plan for facilitating coordination among all agencies and organizations with responsibilities related to missing children; identify and summarize effective models of cooperation; identify and summarize effective programs for victims of abduction; and describe in detail the activities in the national resource center and clearinghouse, among other requirements; —Requires the OJJDP Administrator to disseminate information about free or low-cost legal, restaurant, lodging, and transportation services available for the families of missing children, as well as information about the lawful use of school records and birth certificates to identify and locate missing children; —Requires the OJJDP Administrator to establish annual research, demonstration, and service program priorities for making grants and contracts, and criteria based on merit for making such grants and contracts; limits a grant or contract to $50,000 unless the grant is competitive; —Provides funding authorization at such sums as necessary for FY1989 through FY1992.
1989 (P.L. 101-204)	Technical amendments only.
1992 (P.L. 102-586)	Provides funding authorization at such sums as necessary for FY1993 through FY1996.
1994 (P.L. 103-322)	Establishes a task force composed of law enforcement officers from pertinent federal agencies to work with the National Center for Missing and Exploited Children (NCMEC) and coordinate federal law enforcement resources to assist state and local authorities in investigating the most difficult cases of missing and exploited children.
1996 (P.L. 104-235)	—Requires that the OJJDP Administrator use only up to 5% of the amount appropriated for a fiscal year to conduct an evaluation of the effectiveness of programs and activities under the Missing Children's Assistance Act; —Provides funding authorization at such sums as necessary for FY1997 through FY2001.
1998 (P.L. 105-314)	Deletes the language to establish a task force composed of law enforcement officers from pertinent federal agencies to work with NCMEC.

Year (Public Law)	Description
1999 (P.L. 106-71)	—Provides an annual grant to NCMEC to carry out the activities originally designated to the OJJDP Administrator, including the following: (1) operate the national 24-hour, toll-free telephone line, (2) coordinate the operation of the telephone line with the operation of the Runaway and Homeless Children Program's national communications system, and (3)operate the official national resource center and information clearinghouse for missing and exploited children, among other responsibilities; —Requires the OJJDP Administrator to make grants to or enter into contracts to periodically conduct national incidence studies to determine for a given year the actual number of children reported missing, among other statistics; and —Provides funding authorization for NCMECat $10 million for FY2000 through FY2003 and such sums as necessary for the Missing Children's Assistance Act program for these same years.
2003 (P.L. 108-21)	—Provides funding authorization for NCMECat $20 million for FY2004 through FY2005; and —Provides that NCMEC coordinate the operation of a cyber tipline to provide online users an effective means of reporting Internet-related child sexual exploitation in the areas of distribution of child pornography, online enticement of children for sexual acts, and child prostitution.
2003 (P.L. 108-96)	Provides funding authorization for NCMEC at $20 million for FY2004 through FY2008 and such sums as necessary for the Missing Children's Assistance Act program for these same years.
2006 (P.L. 109-248)	Changes the definition of missing child to any individual less than 18 years of age whose whereabouts are unknown to such individual's legal guardian.
2008 (P.L. 110-240)	Provides funding authorization for NCMEC at $40 million for FY2008 and such sums as necessary for FY2009 through FY2013, and such sums as necessary for the Missing Children's Assistance Act program for these same years. The law also authorizes the OJJDP Administrator to make the grant to NCMEC to carry out specified activities, some of which were already carried out by the organization before the law was enacted.
2008 (P.L. 110-344)	Provides authority to an Inspector General to authorize staff to assist NCMEC by conducting reviews of inactive case files to develop recommendations for further investigations and by engaging in similar activities.

Table A-1. (Continued)

Year (Public Law)	Description
2013 (P.L. 113-38)	Provides funding authorization of $40 million for each of FY2014 through FY2018 for OJJDP to fund activities carried out under the act. Of this amount, up to $32.2 million is tobe used for NCMEC. The law also requires more regular (every three years) studies on missing and sexually exploited children and implements new accountability standards for grant recipients.

Source: Compiled by the Congressional Research Service (CRS).

Notes: This compilation only includes amendments to the Missing Children's Assistance Act, which outlines the duties of OJJDP and NCMEC. The act is codified at 34 U.S.C. 11293 et seq. (Chapter 111, Juvenile Justice and Delinquency Prevention). In addition to funding for NCMEC and selected other activities, the Missing and Exploited Children's program supports the Internet Crimes Against Children (ICAC) Task Force program and the AMBER Alert program. The ICAC Task Force program is codified at 34 U.S.C. §§21112-21117 (Chapter 211, Combating Child Exploitation) and was authorized under the PROTECT Our Children Act of 2008 (P.L. 110- 401), as amended. The AMBER Alert program is codified at 34 U.S.C. §20501 (Chapter 205, AMBER Alert) and was authorized under the PROTECT Act (P.L. 108-21).

The program additionally supports program administration, printing of publications for Missing Children's Day,[55] and grant programs that vary from year to year. For example, the program contributed funding to a DOJ mentoring grant in FY2017 that focuses on mentoring for child victims of commercial sexual exploitation and domestic trafficking.[56] This grant was administered as part of the DOJ Mentoring program.

[55] See DOJ, OJP, OJJDP, "About Missing Children's Day," https://www.ojjdp.gov/missingchildrensday/.

[56] See, DOJ, OJP, OJJDP, OJJDP FY 2017 Mentoring for Child Victims of Commercial Sexual Exploitation and Domestic Sex Trafficking Initiative, https://www.ojjdp.gov/grants/solicitations/FY2017/CVCSEDSMent.pdf.

In: Children's Issues and Legislation ISBN: 978-1-53614-493-2
Editor: Christie Nguyen

Chapter 5

DEFERRED ACTION FOR CHILDHOOD ARRIVALS (DACA): FREQUENTLY ASKED QUESTIONS*

Andorra Bruno

SUMMARY

On September 5, 2017, Attorney General Jeff Sessions announced that the Deferred Action for Childhood Arrivals (DACA) policy, an Obama Administration initiative, was being rescinded. A related memorandum released by the Department of Homeland Security (DHS) that same day rescinded the 2012 memorandum that established DACA and described how DHS would "execute a wind-down of the program." According to the September 2017 memorandum, DHS will continue to adjudicate certain DACA requests and will not terminate previously issued grants of deferred action or employment authorization "solely based on the directives in this memorandum."

---

* This is an edited, reformatted and augmented version of Congressional Research Service, Publication No. R44764, dated September 6, 2017.

DACA was established in June 2012, when DHS announced that certain individuals without a lawful immigration status who were brought to the United States as children and met other criteria would be considered for temporary relief from removal. To request DACA (initial or renewal), an individual has to file specified forms with DHS's U.S. Citizenship and Immigration Services (USCIS) and pay associated fees. USCIS's decision on an initial DACA request or a renewal request is discretionary. DACA recipients are not granted a lawful immigration status and are not put on a pathway to a lawful immigration status. They are, however, considered to be lawfully present in the United States during the period of deferred action.

Cumulatively, through March 31, 2017, USCIS approved 787,580 initial DACA requests and 799,077 renewal requests. The overall approval rates for DACA requests accepted and decided by March 31, 2017, were approximately 92% for initial requests and 99% for renewals.

To date, Congress has considered, but never enacted, legislation on the DACA initiative. Several bills introduced in the 115th Congress would provide different forms of immigration protection to unauthorized childhood arrivals who satisfy specified eligibility criteria. Some of these bills would provide temporary protection from removal and employment authorization to eligible individuals, while other measures would establish pathways for eligible individuals to become U.S. lawful permanent residents (LPRs).

This report provides answers to frequently asked questions about the DACA initiative.

INTRODUCTION

On September 5, 2017, Attorney General Jeff Sessions announced that Deferred Action for Childhood Arrivals (DACA), an Obama Administration initiative, was being rescinded. A related memorandum[1]

---

[1] U.S. Department of Homeland Security, Memorandum to James W. McCament, Acting Director, U.S. Citizenship and Immigration Services, Thomas D. Homan, Acting Director, U.S. Immigration and Customs Enforcement, Kevin K. McAleenan, Acting Commissioner, U.S. Customs and Border Protection, Joseph B. Maher, Acting General Counsel, Ambassador James D. Nealon, Assistant Secretary, International Engagement, Julie M. Kirchner, Citizenship and Immigration Services Ombudsman, from Elaine C. Duke, Acting Secretary of Homeland Security, Rescission of the June 15, 2012 Memorandum Entitled "Exercising Prosecutorial Discretion with Respect to Individuals Who Came to the United States as Children," September 5, 2017, https://www.dhs.gov/news/2017/09/05/ memorandum-rescissiondaca.

released by the Department of Homeland Security (DHS) that same day rescinded the 2012 memorandum[2] that established the DACA process. DACA was created to provide temporary relief from removal from the United States for individuals without a lawful immigration status who were brought to the United States as children and met other criteria.[3] Under the DACA process, both initial grants of deferred action and renewals are issued for a period of two years.

In addition to rescinding the 2012 DACA memorandum, the September 2017 memorandum states that DHS will "execute a wind-down" of DACA, during which it will "adjudicate certain requests for DACA and associated applications meeting certain parameters." These requests include initial and renewal requests for DACA accepted by DHS by September 5, 2017, and renewal requests from current DACA beneficiaries whose benefits will expire between September 5, 2017, and March 5, 2018, and whose renewal requests are accepted by DHS by October 5, 2017. The memorandum also states that DHS will not terminate previously issued grants of deferred action or employment authorization "solely based on the directives in this memorandum."

To provide context for the Trump Administration's rescission of DACA and possible congressional action, this report addresses frequently asked questions about the DACA initiative.

---

2 U.S. Department of Homeland Security, Memorandum to David V. Aguilar, Acting Commissioner, U.S. Customs and Border Protection, Alejandro Mayorkas, Director, U.S. Citizenship and Immigration Services, John Morton, Director, U.S. Immigration and Customs Enforcement, from Janet Napolitano, Secretary of Homeland Security, "Exercising Prosecutorial Discretion with Respect to Individuals Who Came to the United States as Children," June 15, 2012, http://www.dhs.gov/xlibrary/assets/s1-exercising-prosecutorial-discretion-individuals-who-came-to-us-as-children.pdf.

3 DACA is a form of deferred action. U.S. Citizenship and Immigration Services (USCIS) describes deferred action as "a use of prosecutorial discretion to defer removal action against an individual for a certain period of time." U.S. Department of Homeland Security, U.S. Citizenship and Immigration Services, Consideration of Deferred Action for Childhood Arrivals, https://www.uscis.gov/humanitarian/consideration-deferred-action-childhood-arrivals-daca.

How Was DACA Established?

The DACA initiative was announced by former DHS Secretary Janet Napolitano in a June 15, 2012, DHS memorandum entitled, "Exercising Prosecutorial Discretion with Respect to Individuals Who Came to the United States as Children." The DACA initiative was not established by executive order.

What Are the Eligibility Requirements for Consideration of DACA?

The eligibility criteria are

- under age 16 at the time of entry into the United States;
- under age 31 on June 15, 2012;
- continuous residence in the United States for at least five years before June 15, 2012 (that is, since June 15, 2007);
- physical presence in the United States on June 15, 2012, and at the time of making the request for consideration of deferred action;
- not in lawful immigration status on June 15, 2012;
- not convicted of a felony, a significant misdemeanor, or three or more misdemeanors, and not otherwise a threat to national security or public safety; and
- in school, graduated from high school or obtained general education development certificate, or honorably discharged from the U.S. Armed Forces or the Coast Guard.

In addition, an individual must be at least age 15 to request DACA, unless he or she is in removal proceedings or has a final removal order or voluntary departure order.

What Forms and Other Materials Must an Individual Have Filed to Request Consideration of DACA?

An individual must have filed the following three forms with DHS's U.S. Citizenship and Immigration Services (USCIS):

- Form I-821D, Consideration of Deferred Action for Childhood Arrivals
- Form I-765, Application for Employment Authorization
- Form I-765WS, Worksheet

The individual also should have submitted evidence that he or she met the DACA eligibility requirements (see "What are the eligibility requirements for consideration of DACA?").

Was There a Fee to Request Consideration of DACA?

Yes. The fees, which most recently totaled $495, consisted of a Form I-765 filing fee of $410 and biometric services fee of $85.

There were limited fee exemptions available. An individual musthave requested and received a fee exemption before submitting a DACA request without a fee.

Are DACA Applicants Subject to Background Checks?

Yes. The biographic and biometric information submitted by applicants is checked against databases maintained by DHS and other federal agencies.

Is the Information Provided by DACA Applicants Protected?

According to DHS, information provided in a DACA request generally "will not be proactively provided to other law enforcement entities (including ICE and CBP) for the purpose of immigration enforcement proceedings unless the requestor poses a risk to national security or public safety" or meets certain criteria.[4] At the same time, DHS maintains the following:

This policy, which may be modified, superseded, or rescinded at any time without notice, is not intended to, does not, and may not be relied upon to create any right or benefit, substantive or procedural, enforceable by law by any party in any administrative, civil, or criminal matter.

If an Individual Satisfies the Eligibility Requirements, Is DACA Automatically Granted?

No. USCIS's decision on a DACA request is discretionary.

Can an Individual Who Has Never Requested Consideration of DACA Still Do So, or Has the Period for Filing Initial DACA Requests Closed?

The period has closed. USCIS stopped accepting initial DACA requests as of September 5, 2017. However, the agency will reportedly adjudicate initial requests for DACA accepted by that date.

---

[4] U.S. Department of Homeland Security, Frequently Asked Questions: Rescission Of Deferred Action For Childhood Arrivals (DACA), September 5, 2017, answer to Q8, https://www.dhs.gov/news/2017/09/05/frequently-askedquestions-rescission-deferred-action-childhood-arrivals-daca (hereinafter cited as DHS, 2017 DACA FAQs). ICE is DHS's Immigration and Customs Enforcement; CBP is DHS's Customs and Border Protection.

Are DACA Recipients Legally Allowed to Work?

Individuals granted deferred action may receive work authorization if they can demonstrate an economic necessity for employment.

Are DACA Recipients Allowed to Travel Outside the United States?

Previously, an individual granted deferred action under DACA who wanted to travel outside the United States could apply to USCIS for advance parole. Advance parole is permission for a foreign national to re-enter the United States after temporarily traveling abroad.[5] USCIS, however, is no longer approving advance parole requests associated with DACA. At the same time, the September 2017 DHS memorandum stated that DHS "will generally honor the validity period for previously approved applications for advance parole."

ARE DACA RECIPIENTS ELIGIBLE FOR FEDERAL PUBLIC BENEFITS?

DACA recipients, like other foreign nationals without lawful immigration status, are barred from receiving federal public benefits with the exception of certain forms of short-term, emergency assistance.[6]

---

[5] Advance parole, however, does not guarantee re-entry into the United States; foreign nationals are subject to inspection at U.S. ports of entry and may be denied entry.

[6] See CRS Report RL33809, Noncitizen Eligibility for Federal Public Assistance: Policy Overview.

Are DACA Recipients Granted Lawful Immigration Status?

No. DACA recipients are not granted a lawful immigration status and are not put on a pathway to a lawful immigration status. During the period of deferred action, however, the DACA recipient is in a period of stay authorized by DHS.

Can an Individual's Deferred Action Under DACA Be Terminated Before the End of the Two-Year DACA Grant Period?

Presumably, yes. According to DHS, the agency "will continue to exercise its discretionary authority to terminate or deny deferred action at any time when immigration officials determine termination or denial of deferred action is appropriate."[7]

What Requirements Must a DACA Recipient Meet in Order to Be Considered for Renewal of DACA?

The DACA recipient must satisfy the following criteria:

- the individual did not depart from the United States on or after August 15, 2012, without first obtaining advance parole (see "Are DACA recipients allowed to travel outside the United States?");
- the individual has continuously resided in the United States since submitting his or her latest approved DACA request; and

[7] DHS, 2017 DACA FAQs, answer to Q9.

- the individual has not been convicted of a felony, a significant misdemeanor, or three or more misdemeanors, and is not a threat to national security or public safety.

According to DHS, it will accept renewal requests from eligible DACA recipients until October 5, 2017 (see "Introduction").

What Forms and Other Materials Does an Applicant for DACA Renewal Have to File?

To request a renewal of deferred action under DACA, an individual must file the following three forms with DHS/USCIS:

- Form I-821D, Consideration of Deferred Action for Childhood Arrivals
- Form I-765, Application for Employment Authorization
- Form I-765WS, Worksheet

The forms are available on the USCIS website, http://www. uscis.gov.

An individual requesting a DACA renewal does not have to submit any documents that he or she previously provided to USCIS in connection with an approved DACA request. However, the individual does have to submit any new documents related to removal proceedings or criminal history. USCIS will request additional documentation from the individual, if needed.

Is There a Fee for DACA Renewal Requests?

There is a total fee of $495, consisting of a Form I-765 filing fee of $410 and biometric services fee of $85.

Is Approval of a DACA Renewal Request Automatic?

No. The decision on a request to renew DACA is discretionary, as it is on an initial DACA request.

If a DACA Recipient's Request for Renewal Is Approved, Is the Individual Granted Legal Immigration Status?

No. An individual granted deferred action (an initial grant or a renewal) is not given a lawful immigration status and is not put on a pathway to a lawful immigration status (see "Are DACA recipients granted lawful immigration status?").

Would a Person Who Loses DACA Be Forced to Leave the United States?

An individual who loses DACA would no longer have the protection from removal that DACA provides. Whether or not the U.S. government would take steps to remove that individual from the country is a separate issue.

How Many DACA Requests Have Been Approved to Date?

As of March 31, 2017, a total of 787,580 initial DACA requests and 799,077 renewal requests had been approved.[8]

---

[8] USCIS DACA statistics are available at https://www.uscis.gov/tools/reports-studies/immigration-forms-data/data-setform-i-821d-deferred-action-childhood-arrivals. Grants of deferred action under DACA are for two years. The same individual may renew multiple times.

What Are the DACA Approval and Denial Rates?

Of all the initial DACA requests accepted by USCIS for consideration and decided by March 31, 2017, approximately 92% were approved and 8% were denied, terminated, or withdrawn. For renewal requests accepted and decided by March 31, 2017, the approval rate was approximately 99% and the denial/termination/withdrawal rate was 1%.[9]

Has Congress Enacted Any Legislation on DACA?

No legislation on DACA has been enacted. During the 113th Congress, however, the House of Representatives passed a bill (H.R. 5272) to prohibit using federal funds to process DACA applications. That bill read, in part:

> No agency or instrumentality of the Federal Government may use Federal funding or resources after July 30, 2014—(1) to consider or adjudicate any new or previously denied application of any alien requesting consideration of deferred action for childhood arrivals, as authorized by Executive memorandum dated June 15, 2012 and effective on August 15, 2012 (or by any other succeeding Executive memorandum or policy authorizing a similar program)....[10]

Have Any Bills Been Introduced in the 115th Congress Related to DACA?

Several bills have been introduced in the 115th Congress to provide different forms of immigration protection to unauthorized childhood arrivals who satisfy specified eligibility criteria. Some of these bills, including the Bar Removal of Individuals who Dream and Grow our Economy (BRIDGE) Act (S. 128/H.R. 496) and the Securing Active

---

[9] USCIS DACA statistics.

[10] See archived CRS Report R43320, Immigration Legislation and Issues in the 113th Congress.

and Fair Enforcement (SAFE) Act (S. 127), would provide temporary protection from removal and employment authorization to eligible individuals. Other measures, including the Encourage New Legalized Immigrants to Start Training (ENLIST) Act (H.R. 60), the Recognizing America's Children Act (H.R. 1468), the American Hope Act of 2017 (H.R. 3591), and the Dream Act of 2017 (S. 1615/H.R. 3440), would establish pathways for eligible individuals to become U.S. lawful permanent residents (LPRs). (These measures bear similarities to Development, Relief, and Education for Alien Minors (DREAM) Act bills introduced in past Congresses.)

Have Past Congresses Taken Action on the DREAM Act?

Legislation known as the Development, Relief, and Education for Alien Minors (DREAM) Act was introduced in past Congresses. This legislation sought to establish a process for eligible unauthorized individuals who entered the United States as children to obtain LPR status. DREAM Act provisions were introduced both as stand-alone bills and as parts of larger immigration reform bills. Although DREAM Act legislation has never been enacted, some measures have seen legislative action. For example, in the 111th Congress, the House approved DREAM Act language as part of an unrelated bill, the Removal Clarification Act of 2010 (H.R. 5281).[11] In the 113th Congress, the Senate passed the Border Security, Economic Opportunity, and Immigration Modernization Act (S. 744), which incorporated DREAM Act language in its legalization provisions.[12]

---

[11] The Senate, however, failed to invoke cloture on a motion to agree to the House-passed DREAM Act amendment, and the bill died at the end of the Congress. See archived CRS Report R40848, *Immigration Legislation and Issues in the 111th Congress*.

[12] S. 744, as passed by the Senate in the 113th Congress, would have established a general legalization program for unauthorized aliens in the United States, with a special "DREAM Act" pathway to LPR status for certain aliens who entered the country as children. The House did not consider S. 744. See archived CRS Report R43320, *Immigration Legislation and Issues in the 113th Congress*.

INDEX

D

E

F

H

I

J

L

M

N

O

P

R

S

T

U

V

W

Y